Signs of Peace

Signs of Peace

The Interfaith Letters of Thomas Merton

William Apel

ORBIS BOOKS

Maryknoll, New York 10545

Founded in 1970, Orbis Books endeavors to publish works that enlighten the mind, nourish the spirit, and challenge the conscience. The publishing arm of the Maryknoll Fathers and Brothers, Orbis seeks to explore the global dimensions of the Christian faith and mission, to invite dialogue with diverse cultures and religious traditions, and to serve the cause of reconciliation and peace. The books published reflect the views of their authors and do not represent the official position of the Maryknoll Society. To learn more about Maryknoll and Orbis Books, please visit our website at www.maryknoll.org.

Library of Congress Cataloging-in-Publication Data

Apel, William D.
    Signs of peace : the interfaith letters of Thomas Merton / William Apel.
        p. cm.
    ISBN-13: 978–1–57075–681–8 (pbk.)
    1. Merton, Thomas, 1915–1968.—Correspondence. 2. Religions—Relations. 3. Christianity and other religions. I. Title.
    BX4705.M542A65 2006
    201'.5—dc22
                                                    2006009462

For Br. Mark
whose generosity of spirit
and love of life
are true signs of peace
and to Jane
whose love knows no end

Contents

Thomas Merton and the Dalai Lama

Foreword

Thomas Merton's journey toward other faiths began early in his life. As a schoolboy at Oakham Public School in England he publicly defended Gandhi in a school debate. At Clare College Cambridge in 1933 he read a book on Buddhism, and then at Columbia he read Huxley's *Ends and Means,* which led him, he writes, to start "ransacking the university library for books on Oriental mysticism."[1] In his autobiography Merton gives a negative impression of this experience, suggesting the most useful thing he gained from it was a relaxation technique to help him fall asleep at night. He was still clearly searching, however. In 1938 he met the Hindu monk Bramachari, and when he asked him for advice on pursuing a spiritual life Bramachari directed him to the classic Christian texts *The Confessions of St. Augustine* and *The Imitation of Christ.* As he was writing his master's thesis on Blake in 1938 he read Coomaraswamy's *Transformation of Nature in Art* and was also delving into the Taoist sages, including Chuang Tzu.

In November 1938 Merton was received into the Catholic Church. Three years later, on December 10, 1941, he entered the Abbey of Gethsemani. During his early years in the monastery Merton's attitude toward other faiths was negative. In *Exile Ends in Glory* (1947) he wrote of statues of the Buddha as "blind, dead, wayside gods of bronze," and in the first edition of *Seeds of Contemplation* he wrote, "Outside the *magisterium* directly guided by the Spirit of God we find no such contemplation and no such union with Him—only the void of nirvana or the feeble intellectual light of Platonic idealism, or the sensual dreams of the Sufis."[2] This statement was removed by Merton in his revision of *Seeds* published later that same year. In an introduction to a French translation of *Exile* (1953) Merton apologized for the book, admitting it lacked "ecumenical spirit."[3] *The Ascent to Truth* also contains negative references to the Zen Buddhist concept of nothingness in comparison to the use of the term in the Christian mystics.

Merton's attitude at this period is hardly surprising. When Merton entered Gethsemani he was still a fairly recent convert, without a great deal of religious background knowledge. His early monastic years were spent acquainting himself with Christian spirituality, preparing for ordination, and then preparing classes to teach first the scholastics at the abbey and then the novices. Although there are occasional references from this period that suggest he is still interested in other faiths, Merton's real study of Zen and Taoism, along with other faiths, began in the mid-fifties. The change in his attitude was brought about by a number of factors, including his changing attitude to the monastery and the world, and his study of the early fathers and the Christian mystics, where he discovered an attitude of far greater openness than that prevalent in the Catholic Church at this time.

It is hard to remember in the twenty-first century just how new the terms *ecumenism* and *interfaith dialogue* are. Certainly, from a Roman Catholic perspective, they were virtually unheard of prior to the Second Vatican Council, just forty years ago. Yet, prior to the Second Vatican Council, Merton had begun dialoguing with other Christian denominations—Baptist, Methodist, and Presbyterian—and gradually expanded that dialogue further to include other faiths—Buddhism, Hinduism, Islam, and Judaism.

Merton's initial ecumenical contacts at the abbey began in 1958. A group of church history students from Vanderbilt University in Nashville began visiting Gethsemani by arrangement with Dom James Fox in 1955. In 1958 Merton became involved with the group and spent the afternoon with them in the guest house—answering their questions about monasticism. Merton was also somewhat critical in what he said of the institutional church, and this, along with the fact that he brought with him a copy of the Revised Standard Version of the Bible, delighted the visitors.[4] Other visitors began to come from Lexington Theological Seminary; from the Southern Baptist Seminary and the Presbyterian Seminary, both in Louisville; and from Asbury Methodist Seminary. A cinder-block building was erected in the woods about a mile from monastery for these ecumenical dialogues.

Merton's approach to ecumenical dialogue was centered on the religious experience of others rather than on the doctrinal expression of their traditions. In this way he could read or communicate with others whose doctrinal positions differed from his own. Merton writes of this approach in a passage in *Conjectures of a Guilty Bystander:*

> If I can unite *in myself* the thought and the devotion of Eastern and Western Christendom, the Greek and the Latin Fathers, the Russians with the Spanish mystics, I can prepare in myself the reunion of divided Christians. From that secret and unspoken unity in myself can eventually come a visible and manifest unity of all Christians. . . . We must contain all divided worlds in ourselves and transcend them in Christ.[5]

In recent years official statements from the Catholic Church have affirmed the experiential approach Merton took to interfaith dialogue. The Pontifical Council for Interreligious Dialogue in its 1991 document *Dialogue and Proclamation* suggested four forms of dialogue; alongside life, action, and theological exchange, the fourth category was "the dialogue of religious experience." This was described in words very applicable to the approach Merton had been taking thirty years earlier, where "persons, rooted in their own religious traditions, share their spiritual riches, for instance with regard to prayer and contemplation" (*Dialogue and Proclamation*, no. 42).

As Merton's attitude to the world changed, so his attitude to other Christians, and other faiths, broadened. He expresses this change clearly in *Conjectures*, where he writes:

> The more I am able to affirm others, to say "yes" to them in myself, by discovering them in myself and myself in them, the more real I am. I am fully real if my own heart says *yes* to *everyone*.
>
> I will be a better Catholic, not if I can *refute* every shade of Protestantism, but if I can affirm the truth in it and still go further.[6]

Merton goes on to enlarge his understanding here even further:

> So, too, with the Muslims, the Hindus, the Buddhists, etc. This does not mean syncretism, indifferentism, the vapid and careless friendliness that accepts everything by thinking of nothing. There is much that one cannot "affirm" and "accept," but first one must say "yes" where one really can.
>
> If I affirm myself as a Catholic merely by denying all that is Muslim, Jewish, Protestant, Hindu, Buddhist, etc., in the end I will find that there is not much left for me to affirm as a Catholic: and certainly no breath of the Spirit with which to affirm it.[7]

By 1961, in an essay later published in *Mystics and Zen Masters* as "Love and Tao," Merton wrote:

> At least this much can and must be said: the "uni-
> versality" and "catholicity" which are essential to
> the Church necessarily imply an ability and a readi-
> ness to enter into dialogue with all that is pure, wise,
> profound and humane in every kind of culture. In
> this one sense at least a dialogue with Oriental wis-
> dom becomes necessary. A Christian culture that is
> not capable of such a dialogue would show, by that
> very fact, that it lacked catholicity.

This is a far cry from the attitude he expressed in some of his
earlier writings.

Merton's approach to other faiths can be summed up most
succinctly in the words the Hindu scholar Amiya Chakravarty wrote
to him, "The absolute rootedness of your faith makes you free to
understand other faiths."[8] Or again, by a similar comment from
the Chinese scholar John Wu, "You are so deeply Christian that
you cannot help touching the vital springs of other religions."[9]

These words are reminiscent of the Dalai Lama's experience
of meeting Merton in Dharamsala in November 1968, just days
before his death in Bangkok. Reflecting on that meeting many
years later, the Dalai Lama could say of Merton:

> As for myself, I always consider myself as one of
> his Buddhist brothers. So, as a close friend—or as
> his brother—I always remember him, and I always
> admire his activities and his lifestyle. Since my meet-
> ing with him, and so often when I examine myself,
> I really follow some of his examples. . . . And so for
> the rest of my life, the impact of meeting him will
> remain until my last breath. I really want to state
> that I make this commitment, and this will remain
> until my last breath.[10]

I am frequently asked what Merton would be writing or saying if he were alive today. Sadly, I think he would be saying much the same things he was writing forty years ago. Our advances in technology and communication have not necessarily led to deeper understanding, unity, and ultimately true communion among people. In *Signs of Peace: The Interfaith Letters of Thomas Merton* William Apel explores the Dalai Lama's statement about Merton as he mines the deep and rich letters Merton wrote to Christians of other denominations and, beyond that, to those of other faiths. Through these letters both Merton and Apel remind us of that hidden ground of love, that spark in the soul, which is in each and every one of us.

—PAUL M. PEARSON

Preface

Signs of Peace

During the last decade of his life the well-known Trappist monk and celebrated American writer Thomas Merton (1915–68) corresponded with numerous people around the globe about world religions and the need for interreligious understanding. This corpus of correspondence can rightfully be called the interfaith letters of Thomas Merton. His epistolary friends in these exchanges included Protestants, Jews, Muslims, Hindus, and Buddhists—as well as fellow Catholics.

It is the aim of this present work to introduce a representative collection of these interfaith letters and their authors to Merton's reading public and to all those concerned with the advancement of understanding and friendship within the world's enduring religious traditions. My desire is to explore the importance of this correspondence for Merton's life and thought, and to examine the lessons these interfaith letters have to teach us today in the unfinished business of achieving mutual respect and appreciation for one another within the world's great religions. Given the precarious nature of our present world situation, a recovery of the many spiritual insights from Merton and his interfaith friends is most timely. Indeed, a careful examination of these "interfaith letters" discloses just how prophetic Merton and his correspondents were in finding true common ground within the depths of their religious experiences.

Merton deeply believed that the time was long overdue for
men and women of good will from various religious traditions to
step forward and create a climate for the kind of peace and unity
the world had not yet known. In this sense what follows serves as
a primer for peacemaking. How this might be accomplished is
set forth by Merton in a letter dated January 13, 1961, to Dona
Luisa Coomaraswamy, the widow of the great Hindu world scholar
Ananda Coomaraswamy.[1] Merton's words to her help set the
tone and direction for this present work:

> I believe that the only really valid thing that can be
> accomplished in the direction of world peace and
> unity at this moment is the preparation of the way
> by the formation of men who, isolated, perhaps
> not accepted or understood by any "movement,"
> are able to unite in themselves and experience in
> their own lives all that is best and most true in the
> numerous spiritual traditions.[2]

Merton himself was making every effort to follow this advice in
his own life. Especially in the last years of his life the monk of
Gethsemani sought to embrace that which was "best and most
true in the numerous spiritual traditions."

Brother Patrick Hart, who has edited so much of Merton's
work, claims that in his mature years Merton became the "ecumenical monk."[3] According to Hart, Merton, like Saint Paul, "was
convinced that he must 'become all things to all men'—that he
might become a 'universal man'—in the sense of sharing in some
measure the lot of the Jew, the Hindu, the Buddhist, the Muslim."[4] Brother Patrick recalls that Merton made these comments
to a group of his fellow monks following a stimulating day spent
in dialogue with Asian, African, and European journalists who
had visited Gethsemani while studying at Indiana University. Such
experiences, multiplied many times over, convinced Merton of

his calling to expand his spiritual horizons beyond their previous limitations—becoming more and more universal in outlook until he was able to take the "other" into himself. All the while he remained the monk of Gethsemani, centered in his monastic commitment to Christ, but he also demonstrated a remarkable openness to the great truths found within the spiritual experiences of a growing cadre of interfaith friends.

Merton, the "universal, catholic Christian," was carefully preparing himself to go where few had gone before in relation to the wisdom of the world's great religions: he was ready to reach out, beginning with his interfaith friends, to create a global community of the spirit. He was, however, quite realistic about this pioneering venture. He counseled others not to expect too much too soon. But a new age was emerging; it was time to step forward.

Merton near the close of his life was convinced that God was calling forth a new kind of person—someone who could honestly, and with spiritual integrity, embrace the truth and wisdom of more than one religious tradition. This "vocation of unity," as Christine Bochen has called it, was all-consuming in Merton's later work and thought.[5]

In his interfaith letter to Dona Luisa Coomaraswamy mentioned earlier, Merton reveals a clear picture of what was on his heart and mind early in the 1960s. He was on the hunt for those who might join him in his vocation of unity. This nascent vision fired his own spiritual quest to the very end; it is presupposed on every page of the unfinished Asian journey. As a mystic and a prophet he was searching for other "universal" men and women who he knew were already out there in the world somewhere. He wrote:

> Such men can become as it were "sacraments" or signs of peace, at least. They can do much to open the minds of their contemporaries to receive, in the

future, new seeds of thought. Our task is one of
very remote preparation, a kind of arduous and
unthankful pioneering.[6]

I believe nothing was more important to Merton at the close of
his life than this remote preparation of those—himself included—
who were becoming interfaith signs of peace. For only then, in
Merton's way of thinking, could a world so badly torn by hatred
and violence begin the process of healing and reconciliation.

The interfaith letters that we are about to explore are all about
planting the new seeds of thought mentioned by Merton in the
quotation above. He, and his interfaith correspondents, in the
process of sowing such seeds, offered themselves as signs of
peace for a new world as yet to be realized. There is much to
learn from these early pioneers of interreligious understanding
and advocates of international peacemaking. The wisdom that
they share, and the experience of their lives, can do much to
move us forward toward the world of peace with justice they
envisioned. They truly are signs of peace who can speak a redemptive word into our present world situation. They can also,
as we will discover, nurture our souls so that we might find spiritual strength for these days.

The chapters that follow are arranged to maximize our access
to the wisdom of Merton and his interfaith friends. In the first
place, each chapter, except the first chapter on Merton as letter
writer, is focused on the exchange between Merton and one of
his interfaith correspondents. This permits an in-depth study of
the ideas and relationship shared by Merton and that one other
individual. Often, the interfaith friend has views as challenging
and complex as Merton's.

Second, each chapter identifies a theme common to both
Merton and his correspondent. Such thematic emphasis allows
time for the reader to engage these topics, all important for interreligious dialogue and peacemaking, in a kind of *lectio divina*.

In short, the reader is invited into the reflective experiences of Merton and his correspondents. With this sort of arrangement of chapters, each can be read and studied as a self-contained unit. Thus, the reader can go back and forth among chapters and contemplate their lessons without being tied to a sequential development of chapters. (Merton himself did not think in a linear way.)

Third, located at the close of each chapter (except the first) is the complete text of a significant letter sent by Merton to the interfaith friend discussed in that chapter. The addition of these letters allows us to experience Merton in his own voice, uninterrupted and without commentary or editorial intrusion. The letters appear just as Merton typed them nearly half a century ago (with the exception that obvious typing errors have been corrected). His greeting and closing are also included, although his signature is not.

Upon the completion of each chapter, the reader will know much more about Merton and an intriguing interfaith friend. The individuals in this volume were selected because of the depth and variety of their religious experiences. Doubtless many of Merton's other interfaith friends might have deserved inclusion. (Some, like His Holiness the Dalai Lama, would certainly be included except that no letters were exchanged.) Most important, every chapter in this book stands as an invitation for us to think deeply and prayerfully about Merton's call for us to become signs of peace.

One

Merton's Ministry of Letters

*T*homas Merton was a consummate letter writer. Although he sometimes complained of having to write too many letters, he loved to send and receive personal correspondence. The Thomas Merton Center at Bellarmine University in Kentucky reports that thousands of pieces of Merton correspondence have been preserved, and much of it is indeed personal. His letters include correspondence with individuals on matters of spiritual direction, letters to social activist groups, exchanges with publishers and writers, and dialogue on religion in the modern world (like the interfaith letters). In fact, very little of what Merton wrote was not of a personal nature.

Paul M. Pearson, director and archivist at the Thomas Merton Center, estimates that the monk of Gethsemani wrote over ten thousand letters to some twenty-one hundred correspondents—most in the late 1950s and 1960s.[1] This is in stark contrast to the four letters per year that he was permitted to write when he entered the austere Trappist order in 1941. When Merton's *Seven Storey Mountain* (1948) became a best-seller, the abbot permitted Merton the privilege of sending acknowledgments of the fan mail that arrived at the monastery's mailroom. The young author created a form letter thanking his readers for their interest in his book. This was, at first, thought to be sufficient. However, as William Shannon notes, some letters to Merton sought spiritual counsel and required a more personal response.[2] Thus began a letter-writing apostolate that would continue to grow until the very end of Merton's life.

Many letters (perhaps in the hundreds) have not yet made their way to the Thomas Merton Center and remain outside the scope of official archives. Recently, while lecturing on Merton at my own college, I was approached by a man who placed in my hands a copy of a letter sent by Merton to his wife in the 1960s. At the time she had been a member of a Catholic religious order, and she had sought spiritual advice from Merton, who, as he often did, thoughtfully replied. This, I'm sure, is not an isolated incident.[3] There are surely many letters still out there.

Again, according to Paul Pearson, a growing number of letters to and from Merton have been collected in various university libraries, as correspondents have left their papers to various institutions. Examples would include Ed Rice to Georgetown, Dorothy Day to Marquette, Jacques Maritain to Notre Dame, Daniel Berrigan to Cornell, and "Ping" Ferry to Dartmouth. Still more will certainly emerge in the future.

By the late 1950s, even before the Second Vatican Council, Merton had been granted greater freedom to correspond with increased numbers of people outside the cloistered walls of Gethsemani. Merton's circle of friends multiplied quickly and expanded around the world. The number of letters preserved is staggering. After spending three concentrated periods of research for nearly one hundred hours at the Bellarmine Archives, I have hardly made a dent in the Merton corpus of letters. William H. Shannon, on the other hand, who has spent hundreds upon hundreds of hours working through this marvelous literary legacy, reminds us that the Merton letters "almost rival his published works" in their volume and importance. He marvels at the diversity of people to whom Merton wrote:

> The scope and variety of his correspondents are staggering. He wrote to poets and heads of state; to popes, to bishops, priests, religious and lay people; to monks, rabbis, and Zen masters; to Catholics, Protestants, Anglicans, Orthodox Christians, and Jews; to literary agents and publishers; to theologians and spiritual activists; to old friends and young ones too.[4]

Shannon observes with great insight that letter writing became for Merton both an act of friendship and a serious literary endeavor. The sheer volume of Merton's correspondence attests to the well-known fact that Merton did nothing halfheartedly. He took his letter writing quite seriously.

In fact, the main channel for Merton's friendships outside the Abbey—and later outside the hermitage—came by post. He maintained, and sometimes initiated, numerous friendships through letter writing. Since his face-to-face meetings with old and new friends were limited, he was greatly dependent on a constant flow of mail. In Shannon's words, "If he wanted to keep his friends, he could not ordinarily visit them, he had to write."[5] It is also true that Merton wrote letters because of his gift as a writer. And he was very good at it! A writer must write, and Merton found himself embracing the genre of letter writing with a passion.

Indeed, early in his writing career (after *Seven Storey Mountain*), Merton was advised by Evelyn Waugh, the famous novelist and editor of the British edition of his autobiography, "to put books aside and write serious letters and to make an art of it."[6] In the end Merton somehow managed to do both: he authored scores of books and nearly perfected the art of letter writing.

With his penchant for correspondence, some have speculated how much more (if that's imaginable) Merton might have accomplished in our electronic age of email and the Internet. But I, for one, am thankful that Merton was confined to pen, typewriter, and "snail mail." His creative artistry, especially his finely crafted letters, might have been seriously impaired without the slower pace of opening the mail, placing it on the desk, ruminating about it, writing a reflective response, and taking it to the mail box. Letter writing and contemplation somehow belong together; they both take time, real time.

Less speculative, and more to the point, letter writing gave Merton a private channel for reflection that was relatively free of the abbot's scrutiny. For many years Merton's outgoing mail probably was read by the abbot, unless marked "conscience matters." This, at times, may have caused Merton to censor himself. But on the whole, his correspondence was free from the kind of close inspection that his writings for publication received from his order's censors. In his letters Merton had greater freedom to express his opinions and formulate his own spiritual insights without worry that his thoughts might be misunderstood or thought to be official Catholic teaching. According to Shannon:

> Merton's letters (as well as his journals) were the only bit of his writing that did not have to be submitted to the censors; hence, he could be his own uninhibited self. That self could be profound, radical in its thinking, witty, and at times hilariously funny.[7]

It is not a stretch to say that Merton's correspondence provides us a window through which to view his most intimate self. His letters were direct and honest and very personable—like Merton himself. They engaged his correspondents in direct, uninhibited conversations; they were more concrete than abstract; they addressed real life situations and were generally adverse to metaphysical flights of fancy.

Although the interfaith portion of the correspondence is yet to be viewed as its own specific genre, much general scholarship has been done on the Merton correspondence. Robert E. Daggy, for example, provided an early summary of the status of publications related to Merton's letters in 1988. In a small volume entitled *Encounter,* which deals with the correspondence between Merton and Zen scholar D. T. Suzuki, Daggy noted that the Merton Legacy Trustees had approved publication of multiple volumes of Merton's letters under the general editorial direction of William H. Shannon.[8] This important task was accomplished between 1985 and 1994: *The Hidden Ground of Love* (vol. 1), *The Road to Joy* (vol. 2), *The School of Charity* (vol. 3), *The Courage for Faith* (vol. 4), and *Witness to Freedom* (vol. 5).

These five volumes are excellent in their selection and editing, but because of space limitations and legal complexities they contain only Merton's side of the correspondence. They do provide excellent summaries of letters received by Merton from various correspondents. Yet, there are no letters, as such, in these volumes from Merton's friends. According to Robert Daggy:

> This fact justifies the publication of the complete exchanges, from time to time, in limited editions. The shorter versions, by retaining the complete texts of both correspondents, however inconsequential or tangential, will have a decided advantage and value and will help to complete the picture of Merton's mastery of the genre.[9]

The publication of *Encounter: Thomas Merton and D. T. Suzuki* by Larkspur Press, in cooperation with the King Library at the University of Kentucky, is a fine example of this kind of limited edition. Another limited edition, *Six Letters,* had already been printed under the King Library imprint and represented a small but important collection of Merton and Pasternak letters given to the King Library.[10]

Of course, Thomas Merton himself was the first editor of a limited edition of his letters. His now famous *Cold War Letters* were selected and circulated by Gethsemani's famous monk in mimeographed form. Merton sent these letters to numerous friends at a time in the early 1960s when he had been forbidden by his order from publishing any further materials related to war and peace. He also managed to place several of these letters in the publication of his book *Seeds of Destruction* (1964).[11]

Other small collections of Merton's correspondence also have made it into print, including Thomas Merton and Robert Lax, *A Catch of Anti-Letters* (1978); Merton and artist Ad Reinhardt, "The Unpublished Letters from Ad Reinhardt to Thomas Merton and Two in Return," *Artforum* (1978); and Merton and Jewish theologian Abraham Joshua Heschel in *Thomas Merton: Pilgrim in Progress* (1983). Also, the Merton–Henry Miller letters, edited by David D. Cooper, have appeared in the Australian journal *Helix* (1984). Finally, W. H. "Ping" Ferry's publication *of Letters from Tom* was privately printed by Ferry (1984).[12] Other published letters include exchanges with Lax, James Laughlin, and Dom Jean Leclercq, and the list goes on.

Of special interest, more recently, is the publication of *At Home in the World* (1995), featuring an exchange of letters between Merton and Rosemary Radford Ruether. Ruether is now widely recognized as a leading Catholic theological voice in the areas of feminism and ecology. This volume contains some forty letters written between Ruether and Merton from 1966 to 1968. In the correspondence Ruether challenges Merton to justify his monastic existence in a world so desperately in need of activist witnesses for peace and justice. Ruether asked how contemplatives like Merton could remain behind cloistered walls when American cities were literally ablaze with racial discontent and American bombs were dropping on Vietnam. Though Merton and Ruether never did come to see eye to eye on their different types of witness, a genuine affection and respect grew as they listened to each other's theological position. Despite all their differences, they did share the same prophetic concern; Merton, the monk, and Ruether, the activist, both desired a more just and peaceful world. Their strategies and tactics differed—not their resolve.

In the last several years a series published by Fons Vitae on Merton and some of the world's enduring religious traditions has included collections of letters from him to interfaith friends. Examples in this series include such titles as *Merton and Sufism: The Untold Story* (1999), edited by Rob Baker and Gray Henry; and *Merton and Judaism: Holiness in Words* (2003), edited by Beatrice Bruteau. Future work within this series will no doubt give further exposure to correspondence between Merton and those in religious traditions other than his own.

Through all this correspondence Merton had indeed become a master letter-writer. He knew how to get to the core of whatever issue presented itself, and in the process he was able to offer something of his own unique insight. In fact, if we read Merton's epistolary exchanges carefully, we are granted as close a view of the "real Merton" as we are going to get. Here we find Merton most fully revealed, although he is as complex and ironic as ever. William Shannon makes a similar point when he contrasts Merton's letters with his personal journals:

> Merton's journals often tend to be overly introspective and self-occupied. In his journals he is necessarily talking about himself (though he certainly saw the real possibility that these journals would be published). Whereas in his letters he is talking to, and building a relationship with another person. . . . The letters not only tell us what he thought at a particular time; they also show his concern for the effect his letters would have on their recipients.[13]

In sum, Thomas Merton remains most alive to future genera-
tions of readers in his correspondence. Merton's voice can almost be heard as he responds to the immediate concern of a
correspondent, or as he thinks aloud with the reader of his letter
about an observation he wants to share. As readers, we too can
place ourselves in the center of a Merton letter. His uncanny
ability to get at the heart of a matter causes his letters, and those
of his correspondents, to transcend time and place. Merton, because of his attentiveness to self and others, brings all concerned
into a bigger picture—a more organic whole. God's presence
becomes evident to the reader in the turning of a phrase or in a
gesture of true friendship. The letters themselves are often signs
of peace.

In the chapters that follow we observe again and again how
the interfaith friendships that Merton cultivated lead in the direction of peace and reconciliation. Here we have modeled for us a
constructive and highly personal form of interreligious dialogue
and peacemaking. It is a remarkable testament to Merton's gifts
as a letter-writer that he could produce and edit the *Cold War
Letters* at the same time he carried on a worldwide correspondence with interfaith friends. In this regard Merton was not only
in the vanguard of the peace movement, but he was also leading
the way as a pioneer in interfaith understanding. He was fully
prepared to embrace what is best and most true in the world's
great spiritual traditions. Merton knew peace and interreligious
understanding went together. We find such conviction and insight fully expressed in his correspondence. It is to the interfaith
letters, in particular, that we now turn.

Two

Blessings

The Merton–Aziz Letters

*Well, my friend, we live in a troubled
and sad time, and we must pray the infinite and merciful Lord to bear pa-
tiently with the sins of this world, which
are very great. We must humble our
hearts in silence and poverty of spirit
and listen to His commands, which
come from the depths of His love, and
work that men's hearts may be converted to the ways of love and justice,
not blood and murder, lust and greed. I
am afraid that the big powerful countries
are a very bad example to the rest of the
world in this respect.*
—MERTON TO ABDUL AZIZ, NOVEMBER 7, 1965

*I*t is fitting, and very timely, to begin our interfaith exploration with the correspondence of Thomas Merton and
Abdul Aziz—a Muslim and Sufi scholar who lived all his
life in Karachi, Pakistan. The words from Merton's letter to Aziz

printed above could have been written yesterday. As it was, the lengthy correspondence between Merton and Aziz began in November of 1960 and lasted until Merton's death in 1968. Their letters represent for us what Sidney H. Griffith called "one of the most interesting epistolary exchanges between a Muslim and a Christian in the twentieth century."[1]

At a time when there was little or no significant conversation between Muslims and Christians, let alone friendship and understanding, Merton and Aziz appeared to have accomplished the impossible: they met each other on the common ground of their religious experience and became a blessing to each other in spite of formal doctrinal differences. These two interfaith friends never met, but the meeting of their hearts and minds in correspondence (and through prayer) marks a future path for others to follow. Most especially, they demonstrate how we might become blessings to one another. This is an essential, and irreplaceable, lesson to be learned in a world still bent more on cursing than on blessing.

A Personal Word about Blessing

On my sabbatical in 1997 I went to Boston University and its archives to research the unpublished papers of Howard Thurman.[2] Like Merton, he was the author of numerous books, a spiritual guide, a poet, and a social critic. Through his African American experiences his writings explored such universal themes as the self, community, and the search for God (all themes that would have interested Merton and Aziz deeply). I had one week to work in the archives. All week I looked for something that would draw my research together. I hadn't found it, whatever *it* was.

Then, an hour before I had to leave to catch a plane for the Merton archives at Bellarmine University in Louisville, I found it. There before me was an unpublished essay by Thurman about his encounter with a rabbi from Massachusetts named Zalman Schachter—the same Zalman Schachter whose correspondence with Merton can be found in *The Hidden Ground of Love*.

Thurman writes that he was about to begin his spring semester class on spiritual disciplines when a young rabbi appeared in his office doorway at Marsh Chapel. This was the early 1950s and it would have been out of the ordinary for a young rabbi to take a course from an African American Protestant, no matter what his national reputation as a religious teacher. (Their encounter was about as unlikely as the Merton-Aziz connection.) After Thurman acknowledged the young man's presence, without stepping in from the doorway the rabbi said, "I have come to see if I can stand you, and if you can stand me!" Once that was determined, the rabbi enrolled in Thurman's course.

He did well in the course. His papers, said Thurman, were expertly written but unlike those of other students. They were tight, well reasoned, and very orthodox. After a successful semester Thurman thought he had seen the last of the rabbinical student.

Then, it happened again. Standing in the doorway of Thurman's office was the rabbi. Again, he did not enter the office, but as Thurman came out from behind his desk to greet his student, the rabbi fell to his knees and asked Thurman to bless him. This was a part of the spiritual master–student relationship tradition of the orthodox rabbi, but it was foreign to any experience Thurman had ever had.

Thurman reports he remembers offering a prayer, although he has no idea of the words he actually said. Never before had Thurman been asked in such a personal way to be a blessing to another human being. Indeed, they had become blessings to one another at a level beyond their own religious experience and cultural milieu. They taught each other "the things of God." This is exactly what happened in the Merton and Aziz interfaith encounter to which we now turn.

The Merton–Aziz Letters (1960–68)

On November 1, 1960, a Pakistani Muslim civil servant named Abdul Aziz initiated a correspondence with Thomas Merton on the advice of French Orientalist Louis Massignon, who, as a well-known Catholic scholar of Islamic mysticism, had exchanged letters with Merton. Aziz had asked Massignon for "the name and address of some genuine Christian saint, contemplative mystic, so that I may correspond with him in respect to Christian mysticism."[3]

Aziz's initial letter to Merton was rather formal, and certainly polite, as he attempted to establish a basis for contact with the famous Trappist monk. Aziz addressed Merton as "Dear Fr. Louis Thomas Merton" and obviously had been informed about the monk's official name and title within the Gethsemani community. By mentioning their common friend, "Professor Massignon of Paris," Aziz hoped to connect in some meaningful way with the stranger to whom he wrote. Much of the letter then detailed Aziz's study of Sufi mystics within Islamic tradition. Perhaps most important, Aziz spoke of his purchase of Merton's *Ascent to Truth* in 1952 and its value in helping him begin an exploration of Christian mysticism.[4]

Abdul Aziz's attempt to identify interests that he and Merton held in common must have worked, for on November 17 he received a warm and enthusiastic reply from Merton. This lengthy letter begins with a most favorable word from Merton. "It was a pleasure for me to receive your good letter and I am certainly grateful to our mutual friend Louis Massignon for referring you to me."[5] Aziz must have been delighted in opening this letter to realize that his words had succeeded in touching the heart and mind of a potential kindred spirit.

The first step in meaningful interfaith dialogue had been taken: Aziz and Merton had discovered one another at the point of a common interest—the great mystics of their mutual religious traditions. Merton spoke of his interest in Sufis like Hallaj and Rumi, while he responded very favorably to Aziz's interest in Saint John of the Cross. Merton informed Aziz that he would send him some of his own books as well as some materials on Saint John. He wrote enthusiastically about books by and about the mystics of Christianity, which he advised Aziz to obtain from publishers like Harper Brothers.

Before ending his initial letter to Aziz, Merton decided to advance their dialogue beyond a simple exchange of information. Already sensing in Aziz a "spiritual brother," he spoke of the impact of secularism on the modern world. We will return to this topic later in this chapter, but for now it suffices to note Merton's conscious effort to move his discussion and friendship with Aziz forward.

What resulted was a most unusual and dynamic relationship between this Christian monk and a Muslim civil servant. As Sidney Griffith writes in "As One Spiritual Man to Another":

> These letters are rare in that they contain correspondence between a notable Christian and a practicing Muslim in religious dialogue in modern times. Of course, Merton had long been writing letters to scholars of Islam, some of them Muslims. But the letters to Abdul Aziz are uniquely personal and religious.[6]

Indeed, they were letters of grace in which Merton and Aziz became blessings to each other. They met each other through correspondence at a time when each had a genuine desire to learn from others outside their own religions. This mutual desire was certainly a prerequisite for any constructive interfaith dialogue.

Those who study and learn from Merton should be eternally grateful to Abdul Aziz for his probing questions and insights, which, as we shall see, became a hallmark of the correspondence. He caused Merton to think ever more deeply, and personally, about the relation of his spiritual journey as a monastic Christian to that of the Muslim Aziz and Aziz's lifelong interest in the interior life of the Sufi. Aziz, himself, has written about his spiritual connection with Merton:

> My correspondence with Thomas Merton was based on "poverty of spirit," being humble to learn from each other, without display of any scholarship or erudition. . . . Such correspondence, apart from revealing true feelings, also includes spiritual fragrance, especially as the holy names of numerous blessed saints and mystics of Islam and Christianity and their essential teachings have been touched upon therein, apart from the Most Holy Name of Mighty God.[7]

What, then, can be learned from this correspondence based on poverty in spirit? How best can we glean insights from these letters for interfaith understanding today? Four excerpts from the letters will be used to illustrate some of the most important lessons, especially lessons related to what Christine Bochen has called Merton's "vocation of unity."[8] In their commitment to what unifies rather than what divides, Merton and Aziz truly blessed one another—and us.

A World Emptied of God

The first excerpt for consideration is taken from concluding remarks made by Merton in his first letter to Aziz, a quotation that Sidney Griffith also highlights. As one spiritual brother to another,

Merton writes to Aziz of a world emptied of God. In a powerful passage he laments:

> The world we live in has become an awful void, a desecrated sanctuary, reflecting outwardly the emptiness and blindness of the hearts of men who have gone crazy with their love of money and power and with pride in their technology. May your work in Sufi mystics make His name known and remembered, and open the eyes of men to the light of His truth.[9]

Recently, I used this particular quotation in several different talks with Christian ecumenical groups in an effort to speak about the "God behind God" to whom Christian mystics and Sufi saints often point. In a world void of this deeper understanding of the Eternal, we do, in fact, abide in a "desecrated sanctuary." As I made this point, one audience member suggested that much of our conflict today in the world is caused not by faith in the God behind God, but by allegiance to the God in front of God. Settling for the God in front of God creates an idolatry of religion putting *my* God against *your* God—a source of division that divides us all.

In contradiction to this great divide, Merton and Aziz honored the Holy One who stands behind (or above) all institutional formulations of doctrines and dogmas. They knew of a God who exists behind and beyond all organized religion. Both had experienced the true Reality that lies behind all rhetoric. This is what Aziz meant when he wrote that Merton had shared a religious perspective based on poverty of spirit rather than scholarship and erudition. Only at this deep level of experience could ultimate spiritual Truth be found.

Responding to Merton's remarks about the effects of secularism (a world emptied of God), Aziz in his letter of December 20,

1960, told Merton that he was greatly moved by his sentiments and prayed for Merton's "spiritual longevity and advancement in spiritual illumination the very next day." He expressed his appreciation to Merton for the "frankness of your heart" on all these matters. In return, he asked Merton to "pray for my spiritual illumination."[10] Aziz sensed in Merton's remarks that he too sought something much deeper in his spiritual quest than the simple answers the world had to offer, or even the surface answers posited in the formal structures of his own religion. As spiritual brothers they both looked for the God behind God— what Merton elsewhere called "the hidden ground of Love."[11]

The Unity of God

A second excerpt from the Merton-Aziz letters further illustrates the unitive nature of their encounter—to bless is to unite. In this passage Merton attempts to respond to Aziz's inquiry about why the teaching of the doctrine of the Trinity is so essential to Christians. With their growing friendship they had reached a level of discourse that permitted discussion of even the most divisive issues. Merton, on his part, humbly confessed that he was "perhaps not equal to the task of making clear" one of Christianity's greatest mysteries. Nonetheless, he pressed forward with remarkable clarity, trying to speak intelligently about the concept of the Trinity and the crucial Islamic teaching of God's oneness (tawhid).

Attempting to find common ground, Merton wrote the following words in his letter of October 18, 1963:

> Just as you (and I too) speak with reverence of
> Allah Rahman and Rahim (the Merciful, the Com-
> passionate), so I think you can see that speaking

of Father, Son and Holy Ghost does not imply numerically separate beings. The chief thing that is
to be stressed before all else is the transcendent
UNITY of God. Now as this unity is beyond all
number, it is a unity in which "one" and "three"
are not numerically different. Just as Allah remains
"one" while being compassionate and merciful, and
His compassion and mercy represent him in different relations to the world, so the Father and Son
and Holy Spirit are perfectly One, yet represent
different relations.[12]

In this statement it is clear that, above all else, Merton sought to
express the unity of God, which he felt united him spiritually to
his friend Abdul Aziz. However, he does not gloss over differences in theological perspective. In the same letter Merton writes:
"The fact is that we believe, as you know, that Christ is not a
being outside of God who is His helper. It is God in Christ who
does the work of salvation."[13]

Aziz finds this point very hard to accept. It seems to contradict
a major point of Islam, which he had already made with Merton
in his letter of April 4, 1963. According to Aziz:

Islam inculcates individual responsibility for one's
actions and does not subscribe to the doctrine of
the atonement or theory of redemption. The Muslims believe that this was the common faith of all
the true messengers of God right from Adam down
to the last Holy Prophet of Islam, including great
patriarchs like Noah, Abraham, Isaac, Jacob, Jo-
seph, Moses, David, Solomon, and Jesus Christ. It
is obvious that "faith" cannot change with different
epochs.[14]

Here is a major doctrinal impasse, and Aziz properly notes the Qur'an's teaching, which emphasizes Jesus as a great messenger of God but not a redeemer of humanity. Merton also recognized the impasse and wrote back: "As you say, the differences begin with the question of soteriology (salvation). I think that controversy is of little value because it takes us away from the spiritual realities into the realm of words and ideas."[15] The road forward, for Merton, as it will continue to be, is in concrete spiritual experience rather than abstract theological ideas.

In order to move ahead Merton and Aziz register their differences but do not permit them to become obstacles to spiritual kinship. In fact, when Aziz quotes from Pope Pius XI (1857–1939) and his charge to his apostolic delegate to Libya, Merton is quick to pick up on this conciliatory note. Merton supported the pope's historic remark to his delegate: "Do not think that you are going among infidels. Muslims attain to Salvation. The ways of Providence are infinite."[16]

Reinforcing this position, Merton in his letter of October 18, 1963, boldly reasserted his spiritual unity with Aziz:

> I perfectly agree that any man in his heart who sincerely believes in God and acts according to his conscience, with all rectitude, will certainly be saved and will come to the vision of God. I have no doubt in my mind whatever that a sincere Muslim will be saved and brought to Heaven, even though for some reason he may not subjectively be able to accept all that the church teaches about Christ.[17]

Merton responds in openness but still in faithfulness as a Catholic believer. Aziz continues very much as a Muslim believer. Yet both proceed and walk together as committed spiritual friends. They experience blessing upon blessing, bestowed by the one true God.

Never Easy, But Ever Faithful

Another excerpt from the correspondence of Merton and Aziz, which we will explore shortly, presents a necessary word of caution for interfaith encounter. Even when the parties involved know each other well, there can be potential for misunderstanding and hard feelings. The Merton-Aziz letters do reveal a fast and firm friendship, but even this has a chance of being bruised.

After Aziz's first rather formal letter, Merton's warm and generous response quickly changed Aziz's manner of addressing his new friend. The opening of the letters to Merton soon changed from "Dear Fr. Louis Thomas Merton" to "My good friend" or "My dear good friend." Merton's informality had opened these channels. Personal information was shared. When Aziz learned from Merton about a hospitalization in 1963, he expressed in writing a "sigh of relief" that it was not serious and called it a "blessing in disguise," because it gave his friend more time to read.

In a very endearing letter from 1966, Aziz expressed alarm at Merton's description of his eating habits at the monastery. He firmly noted to his friend Merton, "I find your diet most austere." After the age of forty, Aziz advised Merton, one should eat more protein and less starch, carbohydrates, and sugar.[18] Merton could also express, in very personal terms, his appreciation of the friendship with Aziz and his concern for his well-being. In response to Aziz's references to prayers for his Christian friend, Merton wrote on January 30, 1961: "I was deeply touched by your understanding and charity. I value most highly the prayers you have offered and, I hope, continue to offer sometime, for me at the hour of dawn when the world is silent and the new light is most pure."[19] With great joy and expectations Merton affirms the life of prayer they shared. There is such assurance in his words:

There is no question in my mind that the mercy
and bounty of God are very clear in the inspiration
which has brought about our correspondence, and
His angels certainly have their part to play in this.
Let us then in joy and humility take the unknown
good which He is offering us in this increased understanding of our faiths.[20]

Yet, even the "increased understanding" of their faith did not
safeguard against possible misunderstandings. Apparently, in a
letter from Aziz that did not survive, he suggested that Merton
consider chanting passages from Islamic scripture daily—as he
did the psalms. Merton had noted his increased reading of the
Qur'an several times in his letters to Aziz. So, it was a natural
next step for Aziz to make this suggestion.

However, Merton explained this would not be advisable for
him to do. His sensitive and thoughtful explanation as to why he
chose not to chant from the Qur'an demonstrates how one spiritual friend can speak to another in truth with love—directly and
honestly. In a lengthy response to Aziz's recommendation, Merton
first apologizes for his delayed response to Aziz's letter due to his
move to the hermitage, away from his monastery:

Actually here I am in a much worse position to write.
Our monastic rule frowns on much letter writing
and being in the hermitage I must give more time
to prayer and study than before, naturally. Also I
do receive quite a few letters that have to be an-
swered immediately, usually from people in urgent
spiritual trouble. . . . Please understand my situation and I in turn will do my best to reply at least
briefly and in substance to whatever you ask that is
within my power to answer without research.[21]

This being said, and rather diplomatically, Merton gets to the topic at hand—chanting from the Qur'an. After questioning the whereabouts of an earlier response that apparently did not make it to Aziz, Merton is direct and clear about why he won't chant from the Qur'an:

> It would not be right for me to chant the Koran daily, as I do not know how this ought to be done properly, and I would not want to simply go in for improvisation in so serious a matter. It seems to me that here again, my task is rather to chant the sacred books of my own tradition, the Psalms, the Prophets, etc., since I know the proper way of doing this. But on the other hand I read the Koran with deep attention and reverence.[22]

Merton teaches at least three important lessons in interfaith interaction as he explains himself to his dear Muslim friend. First, it is not always the wisest of choices to join in the spiritual practices of an interfaith friend—even if one wants to act in solidarity. Merton's observation that the proper chanting of verses from the Qur'an must be given serious attention, and not be done improperly, is no small point. This shows the high level of respect due to such practices. They should not be entered into casually and without proper instruction. Second, Merton does not want to downplay his commitment to his own spiritual practices, which demand primary attention. He wants to ensure that the centuries-old tradition of chanting his own scriptures is honored. In so doing, he preserves the practice of his own community, which keeps him rooted spirituality. Third, and perhaps most important, Merton affirms the high value of his spiritual friend's sacred ways by signaling that he will continue to read the Qur'an attentively and with great reverence.

Thus, Merton, in regards to all three points, honored both his own and Aziz's spiritual practices while maintaining the unbroken bond of their spiritual kinship. Such can be accomplished when friendships are strong. Aziz, on his part, fully accepted Merton's response and its logic. He wrote that he was unaware of the special techniques for chanting required in Merton's monastic tradition, and that was the end of that. There was, however, one spiritual matter of great importance that Aziz continued to ask Merton to write about, namely, prayer.

Prayer

Merton's response to Aziz's inquiry about prayer is perhaps the best-known segment of the Merton-Aziz correspondence. And it is with this fourth segment excerpted from the exchange that we conclude. To his spiritual brother Abdul Aziz, Merton wrote directly about his prayer life on January 2, 1966. This is something he hesitated to do in his published works, but for a friend with whom he prayed there was a proper spiritual context. Merton could speak from one heart to another:

> Strictly speaking I have a very simple way of prayer.
> It is centered entirely on attention to the presence
> of God and to His will and His love. . . . One might
> say this gives my meditation the character described
> by the Prophet [Mohammad] as "being before God
> as if you saw Him." Yet it does not mean imagining
> anything or concerning a precise image of God,
> for to my mind this would be a kind of idolatry.[23]

In the final analysis the use of precise images for God in prayer would be "a kind of idolatry" for *both* Merton and Aziz. It would sidetrack both from their spiritual journey toward greater unity.

This is not to say that various ways of imagining God are unimportant. One could not imagine Merton without Christ or Aziz without notions of Allah's Mercy and Compassion. However, images themselves eventually drop away until there is only God (or as Revelation declares, "God will be all in all"). Words, even the word *God*, give out at this juncture on the road to unity. Here one enters the Void. There is no voice, no image, no vision, only God. It is this God behind God that Merton and Aziz shared.

Those who desire to carry forward this part of the legacy of the Merton-Aziz letters will find the task quite difficult. Far too often the vocation to unity is blocked by advocates of the God in front of God. In religions like Christianity and Islam, there continues to be a divide. However, individuals like Merton and Aziz, in their correspondence, become signs of peace that anticipate a distant new horizon. They point to a spiritual unity that unites rather than doctrinal divisions that continue to divide. They envision a common future when all will be truly One. This will be the day when the entire earth shall be truly blessed.

This is the first letter sent to Abdul Aziz from Merton, dated November 17, 1960. Many parts of the letter are key to the Merton-Aziz relationship explored above. They show Merton's interest in learning as much as he can about Sufism from his new Muslim friend.

November 17, 1960

My Dear Friend,

It was a pleasure for me to receive your good letter and I am certainly grateful to our mutual friend Louis Massignon for referring you to me. Thank you for your very kind words concerning the *Ascent of Truth.* As you expressed some interest in the things I write I have sent to you under separate cover two packages of books of mine which I hope you will accept as a gift. They include most of those you ask for. *The Seven Storey Mountain* is the original edition of *Elected Silence,* and it is a longer, more complete version. There are some passages on contemplation in the later sections of *The Sign of Jonas* and I also included two little books on monasticism. I hope you can find something in these books that may be of interest to you. As to *Seeds of Contemplation* the reason why I have not added this to the others is, frankly, shame. The book was written when I was much younger and contains many foolish statements, but one of the most foolish reflects an altogether stupid ignorance of Sufism. This I have many times regretted, now that I know much better what it is, but I could not bring myself to send you a book containing such a lamentable error. You will pardon me. If there is to be any further edition of the book I shall have the error corrected and then you will receive the book. I shall write to the publisher about this, as there are many other things to be changed also.

Yes, I am indeed very interested in Husayn Mansur Hallaj, that great saint and mystic, martyr of truth and of love. I am also well acquainted with Jalalu'l Din Rumi who is to my mind one of the greatest poets and mystics and I find his words inspiring and filled with the fire of divine love. I am also tremendously impressed with the insights into the mysticism of Islam that I have been able to attain through the medium of Louis Massignon's writings. I believe that it is of the greatest importance for these writings to be studied and made known everywhere and I am sure your work is one that will be blessed with great fruitfulness. I should be very glad indeed to make known to you any possible sources in western mysticism. In return, if you can help me to widen my knowledge and understanding of Sufism I would be deeply grateful to you. No doubt there are some publications of your own, in the form of books or articles, which you might be able to share with me.

In regard to St John of the Cross, I think we have here some paperback editions of his main works and I have asked them to be sent to you. I might also refer you to the *Life of St John of the Cross*, in French, by Père Bruno de Jésus-Marie, which has some interesting pages on the possible influence of Sufism in the mysticism of St John of the Cross. References will lead you further along these lines. I forget the name of the French publisher, but any one of your correspondents in France can inform you. I wonder if Father Paul Nwyia still has another offprint of his article on Ibn Abbad and St John: I would be very interested in reading it as I do not know this mystic. In fact my ignorance in this field is very great.

Some important books which I recommend to you can be obtained from Harper Brothers, 49, East 33nd Street, New York, 16. Write to Miss Ann Perkins, there, and say that I referred you to her. They are publishing an interesting little volume, *The Centuries of Thomas Traherne*, which you ought to have. They have a long list of excellent things and at your suggestion they might be willing to reprint the Malaval book to which you refer. They print something of Fenelon, I believe. Also a fine book by John Ruysbroeck, the *Adornment of the Spiritual Marriage*. You should also get to know the anonymous *Cloud of Unknowing* of which a new edition has been printed by the Julian Press, 80 East 11th Street, New York 3. St Bernard of Clairvaux, one of the early fathers of the Cistercian Order of which I am a monk, has some very important mystical writings. Perhaps the best way to get to know him would be to read the *Mystical Theology of St Bernard* by Etienne Gilson, published by Sheed and Ward, New York 3. (I think that is sufficient for you to reach them.)

These are only a few of the things that might be of interest and importance in your researches. Do please feel free to call upon me for anything else. I will try to answer any questions in these matters. Or look up any book that you may want, though I am in a very bad position for contacting secondhand booksellers as we are in the depths of the country, surrounded by woods and far from any city.

One question you can perhaps answer for me. Recently in a museum I came across a most remarkable and sacred Islamic work, a beautifully designed cloth that was once spread over the tomb of a holy man, Imam Riza. There was on this cloth a Sufi poem, fortunately translated into English on a notice nearby. I was deeply moved by this sacred object and poem and felt a profound sorrow and distress that it had come so far to be reduced to a purely secular function. Yet I thanked God that I was able in this way to come into contact with a great spirit. I would like if possible to know something about him. All I know I have already told you: his name only. Of course he was from Persia, and a Sufi. The cloth was a thematic representation of paradise, with various animals and four angels. There were also in this same museum fine prayer clothes. It was inexplicably saddening to see these sacred things reduced to the status of mere anonymous objects which no one understands, though the heads of the museum are indeed sensitive and intelligent people and treat everything with great understanding and respect. Yet one is shocked by the awful secularism of our day which has become a pestilence of the spirit.

As one spiritual man to another (if I may so speak in all humility), I speak to you from my heart of our obligation to study the truth in deep prayer and meditation, and bear witness to the light that comes from the All Holy God into this world of darkness where He is not known and not remembered. The world we live in has become an awful void, a desecrated sanctuary, reflecting outwardly the emptiness and blindness of the hearts of men who have gone crazy with their love for money and power and with pride in their technology. May your work on the Sufi mystics make His Name known and remembered, and open the eyes of men to the light of His truth.

With every best and most cordial wish,

Sincerely yours

Three

Love

The Merton–Chakravarty Letters

For a writer there is surely not much that can be more rewarding than the fact of being read and understood and appreciated.

—MERTON TO AMIYA CHAKRAVARTY,
APRIL 13, 1967

*B*eing appreciated is an experience that brings love into our lives. Nothing fuels the human spirit more than being valued and understood by another human being. This is exactly what happened to Thomas Merton when he received word that a "Merton Evening" was to be held by students and faculty at Smith College during the spring semester of 1967. On March 29, 1967, Professor Amiya Chakravarty wrote to Merton and reported how the students and faculty at this Northampton, Massachusetts, campus "were immersed in the silence and eloquence of your thoughts and writings."[1]

Chakravarty marveled at what he witnessed that memorable evening. He wrote to Merton, "The enlightened, spiritually sensitive Smith girls, I find, somehow understand you as much and perhaps more than many of the academics or narrowly theological scholars."[2] This must have brought a smile to Merton's face: he had been heard and understood by those who really matter—the next generation. The Smith students were hopeful and ready to listen and learn. They had become agents of love.

Listening, in fact, is the essential first step in Merton's approach to genuine communication—especially in matters of the spirit and interreligious dialogue. Merton's response to the Smith students through Professor Chakravarty, as we shall see, provides an excellent example of how to listen and respond in love to what is in another person's heart. Merton was convinced that only by learning to listen could "that hidden ground of Love," which undergirds our existence as human beings, be fully revealed.[3]

Only by listening to one another are the bonds of spiritual friendship and personal insight made possible. At the experiential level, such ties, regardless of doctrinal or ecclesiastical differences, can lead to open dialogue and the sharing of "that hidden ground of Love." In this chapter the interfaith friendship of Thomas Merton and Amiya Chakravarty provides an instructive example of how to do this. After all, it was Merton and Chakravarty who helped the Smith students develop their enlightened and spiritually sensitive ways.

Amiya Chakravarty (1901–86)

The friendship between Amiya Chakravarty and Thomas Merton did not begin until 1966, less than three years before Merton's death in December 1968. Born in Serampore, West Bengal, India, in 1901, Chakravarty was educated in his native country at the University of Patna and in England at Oxford University, where he received his Ph.D. in 1936. A member of Phi Beta

Kappa, he later taught in the United States at Boston University, Smith College, and the State University of New York.

As a young man, Chakravarty was literary secretary to the renowned Indian poet Rabindranath Tagore. Chakravarty himself was soon recognized internationally as a poet, Indian philosopher, and world scholar. He engaged in an active publishing career, contributing to the *Saturday Review*, the *Atlantic Monthly*, and many periodicals in India. In 1961 he edited *A Tagore Reader*, which became the definitive English collection of this great Indian poet's work. Chakravarty also authored numerous books in the Bengali language of his homeland.

Chakravarty's interests, however, were not limited to academics and literature. During India's struggle for independence he joined Mahatma Gandhi in his peace marches throughout the villages of India. Later he associated himself in England and France with the scholar and humanitarian Dr. Albert Schweitzer. He also traveled in Africa, the West Indies, and the Caribbean region, surveying multicultural patterns of interaction and addressing problems of religious minorities. His world travels took him many times to Asia, the Middle East, and Europe. Always, his central concern was the promotion of justice and international peace.

Amiya Chakravarty, the world citizen, represented the kind of person Merton would identify as a sign of peace. He, like Merton, attempted to take upon himself what was best and most true in the world's great spiritual traditions. With this perspective he became an effective agent of reconciliation in his day—working tirelessly for a better future for developing nations. He advised the Indian delegation to the United Nations and was highly involved in UNESCO, receiving international acclaim for his work. At heart, however, Chakravarty was throughout his life a teacher—someone deeply committed to the intellectual and spiritual transformation of his students. He wanted them to become world citizens who were awakened to the possibilities for peace and

love at their deepest levels—both in their personal lives and in
international affairs.

The Merton–Chakravarty Letters (1966–68)

Indeed, it was Amiya Chakravarty's loving concern for his students and world peace that led him to contact Merton. On September 28, 1966, he wrote Merton saying that he was taking
the liberty of sending him two copies of *Raids on the Unspeakable.* He hoped Merton would sign these copies for two of his
Smith students who had greatly admired Merton's book. In his
letter Chakravarty expressed his appreciation for *Raids* and the
"enduring contribution" he thought it would make "to literature
and religion."[4]

Raids on the Unspeakable had made a deep impression on
some of Chakravarty's students. They had heard Merton's plea
for a more humane world in a time of war, racism, and violence.
In Chakravarty's classroom teaching, students were learning to
listen carefully to Merton's contemplative voice and its call for
peace and love. Patrick O'Connell's summary of *Raids on the
Unspeakable* helps explain why many college students of the
mid-1960s responded so favorably to its message. Its appeal to
honor the image of God within each human being resonated
with the idealism of young people. O'Connell writes:

> Merton distinguishes the book from its more "de-
> vout" predecessors, though he claims it has been
> "meditating in [its] own way" (1), more poetic and
> less "churchy" than the others, and while not repu-
> diating them, he writes, "In some ways, *Raids,* I
> think I love you more than the rest" (2). He finds
> that its central message is "Be human in this most

inhuman of ages, to guard the image of man for it
is the image of God" (6).[5]

In a time of mistrust of institutions and authority, Merton's personal appeal for spiritual sanity in an out-of-control world spoke
to many college students who were themselves searching for new
ways to relate to the world. There seemed to be a clear sense of
authenticity in Merton's writing—it was not canned or prepack-
aged. Students were prepared to *listen*.

Amiya Chakravarty himself wanted to connect with Merton.
He sought to establish common ground with him. He wrote,
"Though I am not a Catholic, I feel deeply near to the faith."
Chakravarty, in this first letter to Merton, mentioned his pilgrim-
ages to Avila, Assisi, and other places sacred to the church. Beyond this, he wanted Merton to know how valuable his books
had been as spiritual guides for so many of his friends and students. He expressed abundant gratitude to Merton, "Your thoughts
have sustained many of us in these dark hours when humanity is
being driven by violence and terror."[6]

Merton quickly sensed that in this Indian philosopher and poet
he had found a kindred spirit, another interfaith friend. He was
so taken by the spirit of Chakravarty's letter that he wanted to
meet this global pioneer for peace. Thus, Merton opened the
door to friendship and invited Chakravarty to visit him at
Gethsemani, even though by 1966 he had moved from the monastery to his hermitage. The Merton-Chakravarty meeting at
Gethsemani did take place, probably more quickly than either
expected. On November 30, 1966, Chakravarty wrote a rather
urgent letter to Merton asking for a meeting. Soon after they
met at Gethsemani. In their time together Chakravarty sought
Merton's spiritual counsel on how best to be an agent of reconciliation for a family that "by chance and circumstance" had been
brought into "spiritual kinship" with him.[7]

As it turned out, Chakravarty was very grateful for this meeting and the "holy thought" Merton shared. He later wrote to Merton that he found his advice to be "at once loving, critical, and redemptive."[8] Chakravarty felt blessed that he was able to be "an auxiliary part of this prayer for truth and healing."[9] The family in need benefited, but in genuine humility Chakravarty remained uncertain of his efforts in this affair. However, he told Merton, he was willing in such circumstances to trust "the unchanging love that God bears for us all."[10] In a very practical way the interfaith exchange had begun for Merton and Chakravarty. Chakravarty had already made an essential discovery about the nature of their spiritual friendship. It was grounded in love and supported by prayer.

This love, Chakravarty wrote to Merton, was at the deepest level of spiritual experience. It was the love "which Jesus embodies," wrote Chakravarty. He then added, "It is, for me, also the spirit of Buddha's Compassion."[11] In both cases Chakravarty was convinced, as he told Merton, that love had "the quality of transcendence."[12] Indeed, this kind of love and compassion that he saw in Christ and Buddha called for action in behalf of a world in need. Speaking from his Indian spiritual context, Chakravarty told Merton that he rejected the all-too-prevalent view that claimed Buddha's teachings led to a rejection of life or some negative void. On the contrary, true nirvana, said Chakravarty, was best understood in terms of "the quality of transcendence" rather than in the categories of "submergence or extinction."[13] For Chakravarty, the Buddha's ways are life affirming and not life negating. Just as the way of Christ had sometimes been misunderstood in terms of flight from the world, so too, Chakravarty noted, the Buddha's teachings had often been portrayed as disinterest in the affairs of life.

The love of Christ and the compassion of Buddha represented for Chakravarty a clarion call to be agents for peace in this world. Indeed, Chakravarty's insights into Buddhism (as well as Hinduism) helped to stimulate Merton's own thinking in this direction. His views were quite compatible with those of Chakravarty—especially in relation to a positive and life-affirming perspective on Buddha and nirvana. In this regard Chakravarty had a significant impact on Merton's developing Asian consciousness. It is no accident that Merton dedicated *Zen and the Birds of Appetite* (1966) to Amiya Chakravarty.

In one article from *Zen and the Birds of Appetite* entitled "Nirvana," we find some of the fruits of the interfaith exchange between Merton and Chakravarty. Referring to a study done by Sally Donnelly, one of Chakravarty's Smith students, Merton emphasizes the notion of "presence," which he agreed is common to both Buddhism and Christianity:

> The Buddhist ideas of *Dharma* (a word almost untranslatable, somewhat akin to logos) and of *Tatatha* ("suchness") imply a realization of presence, and *Nirvana* is a matter of "pure realization of presence, rather than of absence and negation." The meaning of life is found in openness to being and being present in full awareness.[14]

This idea of nirvana as pure presence rather than as absence and negation is quite similar to the point about nirvana made by Chakravarty in his earlier letter to Merton. Here we find clear evidence of the cross-fertilization that occurred between the thoughts of Merton and Chakravarty. They both want to point to an openness to being that results in full awareness of and engagement with the world.

Merton and Chakravarty had truly listened to each other and learned from each other: "openness to being" led both men to a direct encounter of life. Both had gained a deepened sense of the "quality of transcendence" (Chakravarty's term) within life—not outside life. Whether it came from Christ or Buddha, Merton and Chakravarty agreed that genuine spiritual insight takes us deeper and deeper into life rather than out of life.

This kind of metaphysical discussion, however, was never permitted to remain in the abstract for too long by either Merton or Chakravarty. Metaphysics was valued only if it helped people refocus on concrete ways of being in the world—ways of living a life of wisdom and compassion. Chakravarty must have had this in mind when he wrote to Merton on January 12, 1967. Once again, speaking of nirvana, he noted for Merton's consideration that true nirvana had a touch of what the Buddha called "immeasurable mind" about it. This suggested for Chakravarty a strong "experiential reality" within the message of Buddhism. He considered this reality to be close to the Christian concept of *agape*— a selfless love that, while concrete and quite real, surpasses all human understanding.[15]

In fact, the discussion of these two interfaith friends always seemed to come back to the concept of love. Building upon the mystical idea of being in Christ and loving as Christ loves, Chakravarty linked the limitless love of Christ to Buddha's sense of compassion. To have the mind of Christ meant to love unconditionally. Likewise, right-mindfulness and right action (selfless compassion) in the teachings of Buddha are inseparable in most forms of Buddhism—they too, like Christian love, cannot remain in abstraction.

Merton agreed with Chakravarty's conviction that true spiritual teachings, like those of Buddha and Christ, cannot exist in a metaphysical vacuum, detached from real life. Indeed, he already had made this point in his book on Gandhi, which he mailed to Chakravarty.[16] In *Gandhi on Non-Violence* (1965), Merton notes that Gandhi's spiritual combination of Jesus' love ethic and the Indian concept of *ahimsa* (non-injury) resulted in a creative nonviolent approach to life—one that enlists all of our being. Merton writes that it was for Gandhi "a creed which embraces all of life in a consistent and logical network of obligations."[17]

Both Merton and Chakravarty recognized the soul-force in Gandhi's powerful combination of these spiritual teachings. Chakravarty's response to Merton's book on Gandhi was extremely positive. After all, he had marched with Gandhi, and he recognized in Merton's interpretation of Gandhi the nonviolent way to which he himself was committed. Gandhi's approach, for Merton, was an example of applied metaphysics. He observed:

> Gandhi had the deepest respect for Christianity, for Christ and the Gospel. In following his way of satyagraha (holding on to the truth) he believed he was following the Law of Christ (unlimited love).[18]

Here, Merton had listened to what was best and most true in his own faith—Christ's witness to the love of God for every human being. But he also had listened to Chakravarty's insights into the wisdom of Buddha and the great spiritual witness of Gandhi's Hinduism. In each case the common ground was love, and, like Chakravarty, Merton embraced this deepest of spiritual truths.

The Hidden Ground of Love

It is within this context of love's understanding that we now return to the Smith College students and their "Merton Evening." On January 16, 1967, Chakravarty sent a brief letter to Merton alerting him to the news "that we have decided to have a Fr. Thomas Merton Evening at Smith in February."[19] He told Merton that students in his philosophy of religion course were "most keenly enthusiastic" and that there was "excitement and joy all over the campus" in anticipation of the event.[20] The idea for the evening was to discuss Merton's newest books, his poems, and the Gandhi book. Of course, added Chakravarty, "your autobiographical book will be with us."[21]

Chakravarty concluded this letter by emphasizing his excitement about having Merton's works in the hearts of so many "in these crucial days."[22] Merton wrote back on January 21 thanking his interfaith friend for the good news about "the discussion at Smith." He was obviously delighted but also cautious:

> I feel honored—and also I am not humble enough to take these things gracefully and therefore I am also a little confused. It is perhaps not necessary to do so, but I would like to say that I hope it does not take on the aspect of a personality cult. I think the girls at Smith are wise enough to avoid that. Besides, I have always been frank enough about my limitations for people to be fully aware of them.[23]

This kind of honesty served Merton well, but sometimes almost to a fault. He had had the uncomfortable experience of being idolized by Catholic school children—or at least by their teachers—for his spiritual autobiography. He was adamant about not perpetuating that sort of thing. However, in the balance, he was pleased by the possibilities of such a gathering. He informed Chakravarty, "I am happy with the idea, and it is to me a way of being in contact with others like myself, with kindred interests and concerns, people who look for something more in life than plenty of food, comfort, amusement and money."[24]

Merton was quite clear about that "something more in life" he wanted to share. He wanted his readers to get beyond the materialism of the Western world, which troubled him so deeply. His protest over the Vietnam War and racism at home certainly came into play here. But there was something in addition to all this, something even more fundamental. He wanted to affirm the love of God, which undergirds all circumstances, no matter how hopeless they might appear. In closing his letter of response to the good news of the proposed "Merton Evening," Merton simply

wrote: "May that love grow in all of us. It is the one thing necessary."[25] Like Mary in Luke's gospel, Merton desired for himself
and others only the good portion that cannot be taken away
(10:30–42).

The Merton Evening at Smith College was a marvelous suc-
cess. On March 29 Chakravarty wrote to Merton:

> We had the great evening. It began late in the after-
> noon, but the students and faculty carried on till
> past dinnertime. We were immersed in the silence
> and eloquence of your thoughts and writings. . . .
> The young scholars here realized the absolute
> rootedness of your faith makes you free to under-
> stand others faiths. . . . Your books have the rock-
> like inner strength, which sustains the Abbey of
> Gethsemani, which can challenge violence and un-
> truth wherever they appear.[26]

Chakravarty appreciated Merton's works as a catalyst for the
kind of discussions that could be stimulated on a campus like
Smith. Indeed, Merton's writing, which reflected "the absolute
rootedness" of his faith, let people know exactly where he stood.
At the same time, this kind of rootedness set him "free to understand other faiths" and set others free to do likewise. In short,
Merton set a positive tone for genuine dialogue, and Chakravarty
used Merton's interfaith witness to the benefit of his students.
Clearly, the Smith students had "gotten" Merton. Chakravarty
acknowledges that Merton had been understood at the deepest
of levels. The next generation, at least those at Smith College,
had recognized the authenticity and freedom of Merton's voice.
(One of those students, Diana Eck, is now a distinguished professor of religion at Harvard University.)

On April 13, 1967, Merton wrote back to Chakravarty and
the Smith students. This letter contains the phrase "hidden ground

of Love," which became the title of the first large volume of
Merton letters published posthumously in 1985.[27] In the April
13 letter we find written some of Merton's most inspired words
about God. Once he realized that he had been "really read and
understood and appreciated," there was no stopping Merton.
He was moved to express thoughts and feelings that he could
hardly put into words:

> It is not easy to try and say what I know I cannot
> say. I do really have the feeling that you have un-
> derstood and shared quite perfectly. That you have
> seen something that I see to be most precious and
> most valuable too. The reality that is present to us
> and in us; call it Being, call it Atman, call it Pneuma
> . . . or Silence. And the simple fact that by being
> attentive, by learning to listen (or recovering that
> natural capacity to listen which cannot be learned
> any more than breathing), we can find ourselves
> engulfed in such happiness that cannot be explained:
> the happiness of being at one with everything in
> that hidden ground of Love for which there can be
> no explanation.[28]

By learning to listen to one another, a whole new world became available to Merton and his Smith friends. They saw the
Reality "that is present to us and in us." It somehow managed to
break clear. What Merton struggled to put into words was what
the Smith students and Chakravarty had grasped intuitively. Being or Atman or Pneuma or simply Silence is indeed present all
about us and deeply within us. It is, in fact, "that hidden ground
of Love for which there can be no explanation." It is none other
than God.

Professor Chakravarty, with the help of Merton, had brought
his students into an experience of divine presence. These two

interfaith friends had helped inspire and transform those who represented a new generation. Chakravarty would continue to correspond with Merton about interreligious understanding and the world situation. Both men would also continue to express the need for more spiritual light, a light of love that could shine on the darkness of racism, violence, and war. However, the Merton and Chakravarty spiritual exchange would never again reach the heights of the Smith College encounter.

The Step into Asia

On May 4, 1968, Amiya Chakravarty wrote to Merton, "I do hope you will step into Asia."[29] Chakravarty had received an earlier letter from Merton in which Merton had spoken of a possible trip to Southeast Asia. Then, on June 4, 1968, Merton wrote to Chakravarty reporting that he had received the abbot's permission to make the trip. He told Chakravarty, "Though it is not certain that I shall attend the meeting at Bangkok, I have received permission to go and preach at our Cistercian monastery in Indonesia."[30] The pathway for Merton's Asian journey was now open.

Merton relied upon his friend Chakravarty for addresses of mutual friends who might house him during his travels throughout Asia. Chakravarty, for his part, was delighted that Merton was about to experience the East. In the letter dated May 4, 1968, Chakravarty expressed a special hope that Merton might speak out for the release of the "Buddhist saint" Thich Tri Quang, who had been detained in a South Vietnamese jail for his opposition to the war.[31] Merton, however, had agreed with his superiors to keep his trip low key and nonpolitical. He would travel as a spiritual pilgrim without publicity. He thus had to turn down Chakravarty's request.

Chakravarty was in India when Merton arrived. They met for the last time in October 1968 in Calcutta. Merton wrote in his Asian journal, "Yesterday I drove with Amiya Chakravarty . . . to the home of the painter Jamini Roy. . . . Amiya bought a Christ [painting] which he will take to the nuns of Redwoods."[32] Merton then gave a talk at the Interfaith Temple of Understanding meeting in Calcutta and was soon off to Ceylon (Sri Lanka). Following this, as we know, Merton was electrocuted by a defective electric fan and died in Bangkok on December 10.

Nonetheless, Chakravarty did have one last opportunity to dialogue with his dear friend. This came about when he was appointed consulting editor for the posthumous publication of Merton's *Asian Journal*. In its preface Chakravarty wrote these very perceptive words about his spiritual friend:

COURTESY OF THOMAS MERTON CENTER

Thomas Merton with Amiya Chakravarty,
meeting in Calcutta in October 1968

> Readers of Thomas Merton know that his open-
> ness to mankind's spiritual horizons came from a
> rootedness of faith; and inner security led him to
> explore, experience, and interpret the affinities and
> differences between religions in light of his own
> religion. That light was Christianity.[33]

These very same words could have been used to describe Amiya Chakravarty and his rootedness in the wisdom of his Indian world view, which granted him the openness that Merton so deeply appreciated. Like Merton, Chakravarty was well positioned to explore, experience, and interpret various religions by the light of his own Eastern spirituality.

In this regard Merton and Chakravarty frequently spoke of the power of illumination in their letters. Chakravarty had discovered the light of truth in his interfaith friend. In his travels around the world Chakravarty was surprised to discover how many people had been touched by Merton's writings. In fact, he wrote to Merton in September of 1967 to tell him that numerous people he had met on his international travels had been inspired by Merton's "divinely centered thinking."[34]

Chakravarty also possessed spiritual light. It shines through in his letters to Merton, and it certainly fell upon the path of his students. Merton and Chakravarty were indeed spiritual friends of light. Though darkness was all around, they were constant beacons of God's light, helping to illuminate the dark places. "The light shines in the darkness, and the darkness did not over-come it" (Jn 1:5).

Merton found it impossible, in Chakravarty's words, "to deny any authentic scripture or any man of faith."[35] Merton would have said the same of Chakravarty. When Chakravarty wrote Merton about the "shaft of light" that emanates from Hinduism, Buddhism, and Christianity, he found no disagreement from Merton. As William H. Shannon has said of Merton: "What is important is not Christ as our object of study, but Christ as the center in whom and by whom we are illuminated."[36] Merton saw the light of Christ's love in many places beyond Christianity—including within the spirituality of Amiya Chakravarty.

When we learn to see, as Merton and Chakravarty had, then the light of love begins to shine forth. Whether it emanates from the Smith students or from peasants in Vietnam; whether it shines forth from the monks of Gethsemani or from the religious sages of India; whether it radiates from people at a busy intersection in downtown Louisville or from the poor on the streets of Calcutta; Merton knew, as did Chakravarty, that "they are all walking around shining like the sun."[37] We each are touched by the light of God's love. This is what was of ultimate importance to spiritual friends like Thomas Merton and Amiya Chakravarty—the light that shines deep in the heart of every person, and when discovered, bathes all humanity in Love.

This letter, sent by Merton to Amiya Chakravarty and dated April 13, 1967, is one of the most frequently quoted of Merton's letters. It contains the phrase "hidden ground of Love," which was chosen by William H. Shannon as the title for volume 1 of Merton's letters. The letter includes Merton's delightful response to Chakravarty's report on the "Merton Evening" at Smith College.

April 13, 1967

Dear Amiya:

I have put off answering until a moment of quiet, an afternoon that is almost as hot as summer. And I am answering more than your letter describing how it was when you all talked and read about the monastery and about some of my ideas. I was so moved by the two very understanding letters—from Miss Eck and Mrs. Wilson. And of course by yours too.

For a writer there is surely not much that can be more rewarding than the fact of being really read and understood and appreciated. After all, the great thing in life is to share the best one has, no matter how poor it may be. The sharing gives it value. Often when I re-read things I have written I find them so bad that I am irritated with myself: of course this is only vanity. But once I realize that they have meant something to someone, they acquire something of the other person's value and meaning. What you read and liked of mine I shall like better now because you have all enjoyed them: I will like them because of all of you. I will like them because they are more yours than mine.

It is not easy to try to say what I know I cannot say. I do really have the feeling that you have all understood and shared quite perfectly. That you have seen something that I see to be most precious—and most available too. The reality that is present to us and in us: call it Being, call it Atman, call it Pneuma . . . or Silence. And the simple fact that by being attentive, by learning to listen (or recovering the natural capacity to listen which cannot be learned any more than breathing), we can find ourself engulfed in such happiness that it cannot be explained: the happiness of being at one with everything in that hidden ground of Love for which there can be no explanation.

I suppose what makes me most glad is that we all recognize each other in this metaphysical space of silence and happiness, and get some sense, for a moment, that we are full of paradise without knowing it. Do you read Thomas Traherne? Maybe you would like him.

I am sending along a poem. It is not about this exactly, but it is somewhat along the same lines. But the poem was written before I got the letters and it supposes much younger and more confused people.

Janice Wilson mentioned Ecclesiastes: and of course this is one of the books of the Old Testament I like best. It is in some places almost Taoist. I lectured to the monks about this a long time ago and lost the notes or I would send them.

Well, this is an attempt at answering all of you and saying that I am so happy that you enjoyed reading things I had written. May we all grow in grace and peace, and not neglect the silence that is printed in the center of our being. It will not fail us. It is more than silence. Jesus spoke of the spring of living water, you remember.

On Tuesday the 18th, I will offer my Eucharist for all of you.

With warm good wishes and love, in the Lord,

Four

Wisdom

The Merton-Wu Letters

*I have been for some time persuaded of
the immense importance of a prudent
study of Oriental philosophy by some of
us in the West, particularly in the kind
of perspective that girded some of the
early Church Fathers in their use of
Platonism, and St. Thomas in his use of
Aristotle.*

—MERTON TO JOHN C. H. WU,
MARCH 14, 1961

In the spring of 1961 Thomas Merton was on a search
for a wise man from the East. He was convinced that
Eastern philosophy could make great contributions to
Christianity, much as Platonism had helped shape theology in
the early church and as Saint Thomas had used Aristotle to influence Christian thought in the Middle Ages.

With this in mind, Merton wrote to John C. H. Wu for the
first time on March 14, 1961. He hoped that this modern Chinese sage and scholar might be the person to help him write a

book about the ancient Taoist philosopher Chuang Tzu. This would mark one of Merton's earliest efforts to build bridges between the spiritual traditions of the East and the West.

John Wu proved to be the perfect partner for Merton's venture. His letter of response was immediate and filled with enthusiasm. Wu wrote on March 20 that he was "more than willing to cooperate" with Merton in his project on Chuang Tzu. In fact, he was convinced that Merton's request was "an operation of Providence."[1] Both men, in their own way, had hoped to cross the great divide; Wu from East to West, and Merton, of course, from West to East.

Born and raised in China, John Wu converted to Catholicism as an adult, but he never abandoned the great truths of the Confucian-Taoist-Buddhist milieu of his native land. He was well versed in classical Chinese philosophy and equally at home in the contemplative tradition of Catholic spirituality. Wu was a rare individual for his time—a man for all seasons and cultures. As one admirer noted, "Dr. Wu is one of the most extraordinary personages of the modern world; he has taken all knowledge—East Asiatic and Western—for his province."[2]

John Wu—the Chinese Sage

John Wu (1899–1986) was indeed a wise man, a true modern magus. In his autobiography *Beyond East and West* he writes:

> I often think of myself as a Magus of Christ who
> lays before the Divine Infant in the arms of the
> Blessed Virgin the gold of Confucianism, the musk
> of Taoism and the frankincense of Buddhism.[3]

Wu always considered the religions of China to be "an integral part of the development" of his spiritual life.[4] He believed with all his heart that his Chinese ways were "an important portion of the natural dowry, which God has endowed me in preparation for my marriage with Christ."[5]

This outlook placed Wu in a perfect position to assist Merton. He was open to the wisdom of both East and West but confined to neither. The closing words of his autobiography, written long before his correspondence with Merton, set a direction

COURTESY OF JOHN WU, JR.

John Wu, 1949

for interreligious dialogue that the monk of Gethsemani would later come to appreciate fully. Wu wrote: "Our pilgrimage is therefore neither eastwards nor westwards, but inwards; and this is what I call moving beyond East and West."[6]

There is no mistaking that Merton had found a soul mate in John Wu. Their friendship was instant; it began with Merton's first letter of inquiry in the spring of 1961 and ended only with Merton's Asia trip and death in late 1968. Their correspondence paralleled that of the Merton-Aziz letters in both chronology and volume—over thirty letters exchanged in less than seven years. Wu also met Merton at Gethsemani for face-to-face dialogue during this period.[7]

By the time the Merton-Wu correspondence had begun, the one who called himself a "Magus of Christ" had already become an individual of vast experience and erudition. Not as

widely known as Merton, Wu nonetheless was an individual of
international reputation who had authored numerous books on
jurisprudence, literature, and philosophy. He also had served
his beloved China as a judge and legislator before its fall to
Communist rule in 1949. On the international scene he would
represent the Republic of China as ambassador to the Vatican
and act as an advisor to Chinese delegations at founding meetings of the United Nations. His friends included political leaders
like Chiang Kai-shek and Madame Chiang; in America he befriended the great Supreme Court judge Oliver Wendell Holmes.
In his later years Wu taught Chinese philosophy at the University of Hawaii and served on the faculty at Seton Hall in New
Jersey. It was during his tenure at Seton Hall that his correspondence with Merton began.

Yet, despite all his accomplishments, John Wu's start in life
was very modest indeed. His birthplace of Ningpo, China, was
rather backward and crude according to traditional Chinese
standards. Wu has observed in his autobiography, "There is
something rugged and untamed about Ningponese."[8] Fortunately, however, Wu's family was very supportive. Wu's father
was a respected banker in the community, and he benefited
greatly from his father's reputation as an honest man. But the
greatest influences in Wu's early years were two very special
women.

According to Wu, God granted him not one but two wonderful mothers. He liked to say that he had a "little mother" and a
"big mother." His biological mother (little mother) died early in
his childhood. A second mother (big mother) raised him with
deep affection through his formative years. Wu records in his
autobiography, "If I am asked who of all human beings is dear-
est to me, I would answer without the slightest hesitation that it
is my big mother."[9] She nurtured Wu and encouraged him in
his studies, even though she herself was illiterate.

Uncommon Wisdom

John Wu never forgot his indebtedness to his mothers, the one who gave life and the other who encouraged wisdom. His love of the Blessed Virgin Mary many years later reflects this original sense of gratitude. The adult Wu's special love for the Little Flower, Saint Thérèse of Lisieux, also reveals his embrace of the legacy of compassion he received from his two mothers, who sacrificed so much in his behalf.[10]

Later in life Wu's recognition of the life and wisdom afforded him by his little mother and big mother was to contribute to his theological development. More so than most in his generation, he permitted his theology to be informed by the love that had flowed forth from these two remarkable women. Wu, for example, differed from most Western ways of thinking about God by allowing for the feminine face of the Divine to emerge. His personal experience of two loving mothers, as well as the Taoist notion of the balance of opposites, no doubt led Wu to view God as both Father and Mother. In Wu's thinking:

> God is not only our father, who is supposed to be
> as fearful as the summer sun, but also our mother,
> who is as tender and kind as the winter sun, or the
> autumn moon, or the spring breeze.[11]

Decades before Western theology began to recover an appreciation for feminine images of God, Wu had already incorporated the feminine side of the sacred into his personal theology and spirituality.

In this regard Wu, like Merton, understood that the inward journey of the soul is as crucial for theological reflection as the study of official church teachings. One cannot, and should not, deny the value of lessons to be learned from one's own life story. For Wu, the theological significance of his two mothers could not be ignored. Both Wu and Merton recognized how crucial our own stories are for self-understanding and dialogue—especially when different cultures meet. Wu never failed to grasp the theological significance of his own multicultural story—a remarkable and unique spiritual journey. He writes in his autobiography:

> All my life I had been searching for a Mother, and at last I had her in the Catholic Church and this in a triple sense. God is my Mother, the Church is my Mother, and the Blessed Virgin is my Mother; and those three Mothers have merged in One Motherhood, in which I live, move, and have my being.[12]

This trinity of motherhood made tremendous sense to Wu in both his personal experience and within the spiritual context of his Chinese mind. It provided an alternative view to what Wu experienced as an "unbalanced" perspective among many Western theologians with their overuse of masculine images for God.

John Wu's thinking was uncommon in other ways as well. Frequently, Catholic and Protestant converts to Christianity in China separated themselves from Chinese philosophy and religion—often with missionary encouragement from the West. But this was not the case with John Wu. He remained grateful for the great traditions of Chinese wisdom and continued to draw upon them throughout his life. Even after his conversion to Christianity, he seated much of his wisdom in the heritage of ancient Chinese sages. Merton, in his mature years as a monk, was to adopt a similar approach. He too accepted truth wherever he found it. Looking back, Wu affirmed that his new life in Christ did not cut him off from past wisdom; it enhanced it. He notes:

> Of course, every conversion is due to the Grace of
> God; but there is no denying that in my case God
> used parts of the teaching of Confucius, Lao Tzu
> and Buddha as instruments to open my eyes to the
> Light of the world.[13]

In this regard Wu recalls how he was profoundly influenced by
the school of Buddhist thought called Zen (Dhyana). In his thir-
ties the "mystical tendencies" he had gained earlier from Taoism
"were reinforced tremendously by the study of Zen masters."[14]
Indeed, Merton was to benefit from Wu's understanding of the
spiritual and intellectual connection between Taoists like Chuang
Tzu and the later Zen masters. With great appreciation Merton
was to write an introduction to John Wu's insightful book on this
subject entitled *The Golden Age of Zen*.

Another example of Wu's indebtedness to Chinese wisdom
was his love of Confucius. Like every schoolboy of his generation, Wu was trained in the Confucian classics. And he learned
his lessons well. Wu never lost the love of learning that he inher-
ited from the Confucian tradition. He sounds very much like a
Confucian scholar, when, in his fifties, he humbly admits: "I am
not a learned man, but a learning man. I only hope I shall not
cease learning until I cease breathing." He continues with a wonderful piece of Confucian imagery: "I have a big library, and I
have a nice collection of friends whom I regard as walking books
of reference."[15]

Steeped in this sort of wisdom, Wu reflected on how Chinese
ways of thinking and experiencing the world intersected with
one another. Evaluating the classic Chinese mind in all its nu-
ances, Wu writes:

> Although Taoism is more subtle and ethereal than
> Confucianism, yet compared with Buddhism, it is

still earthbound. Confucianism is ethical, Taoism is
philosophical, but Buddhism is spiritual. It is Taoism, according to a happy phrase of John Dewey,
that colors the way in which Confucianism is received, Buddhism is the atmosphere in which both
of them are bathed.[16]

In sum, Wu states, "such was the physiognomy of the Chinese
soul before the Western influence had taken root."[17] This, for
him, was a rich and bountiful legacy.

The manner in which Wu integrated the various components
of his intellectual and spiritual heritage must have fascinated
Merton. One last example. Wu was confident that the life of the
Buddha had led him to the light of Christ. He greatly admired
Siddhartha Gautama's relentless pursuit of truth; it had a spiri-
tual depth and integrity that Wu truly appreciated. In a passage
from his autobiography, Wu speaks of his path from Buddha to
Christ:

It was these aspirations [Buddha's search for truth]
that jerked me into a kind of spiritual wakefulness
which prepared me remotely to return to God like
the prodigal son. Buddha was one of the peda-
gogues to lead me to Christ.[18]

I am intrigued by Wu's language of being "jerked . . . into a kind
of spiritual wakefulness." Did Merton's familiarity with Wu's autobiography provide the language he later used to write about
his experience of the giant Buddha carvings at Polonnaruwa in
Ceylon (Sri Lanka)? Merton wrote during his Asian journey:

Looking at these figures I was suddenly, almost forc-
ibly, jerked clean out of the habitual, half-tied vision

of things, and an inner clearness, clarity, as if exploding from the rocks themselves, became evident and obvious.[19]

Could Merton have been reminded of Wu's description when he wrote these words in his Asian journal? It is impossible to say for certain, but what can be said—as we shall now see—is that Wu and Merton were to have great influence upon each other's thought.

The Merton–Wu Letters (1961–68)

By the time Merton befriended John Wu through correspondence in 1961, Wu had already anticipated some of the deeper, more inclusive insights in religion and spirituality that Merton was exploring. Earlier we noted that John Wu, in his unique way, drew together East and West in his catholic (universal) Christianity. Already in the 1950s he had concluded:

> It is not fair to Christianity to call it "Western." Christianity is universal. In fact, the West has something to learn from the East, for on the whole, the East has gone further in its *natural* contemplation than the West has in its *supernatural* contemplation.[20]

Merton shared this perspective. Indeed, William Shannon's summary of Merton's approach to a nonviolent and peaceful dialogue with others speaks to how Merton related to Wu:

> [Merton's approach showed] a respect for the humanity and dignity of the other, a recognition that

no one single point of view has a monopoly on the
truth, a willingness to learn from the other, a commitment to truth rather than defending one's position, a "person-oriented" approach that "does not
seek so much to *control* as to *respond* and to
awaken response," which promotes an "openness
of free exchange in which reason and love have
freedom of action."[21]

These essential elements of mutual respect are found in
Merton's initial letter to John Wu, dated March 14, 1961. Merton
wrote of his interest in Chuang Tzu—an interest he knew was
shared by John Wu. From the beginning Merton sought common ground. And he did this in all humility—a first step in Merton's
desire to show respect. Even though he had studied the writings
of Chuang Tzu, Merton carefully deferred to Wu's scholarship.
He knew how superficial many Westerners had been in their
study of the East. Often, this revealed a noticeable disrespect for
Eastern ways. In Merton's words, "There is a great deal of irresponsible and rather absurd dabbling in things Oriental among
certain Western types." Merton said he had no desire to per-
petuate this disservice. Besides, wrote Merton, in a further act of
humility, "I don't want to make myself sillier than I already am by
joining this number."[22]

By making such comments in his initial letter to Wu, Merton
rejected any kind of cultural or intellectual imperialism that so
easily came from the West. He consciously opened himself to
being a learner of Eastern ways. He clearly demonstrated that he
had no wish to *control* the emerging relationship with Wu. In
fact, Merton went out of his way to acknowledge his admiration
for Wu. He writes in the same letter to Wu, "I am familiar with
your books and realize that you are exactly the kind of person
who would be of immense help."[23] With these brief words Merton

affirmed the worth and dignity of his fellow seeker after truth. Above all, Merton wanted to learn the lessons this Chinese sage had to teach him.

In his response of March 20, John Wu demonstrated a similar respect and affection for Merton. He was very supportive of Merton's attempt to better understand the wisdom of the East—especially the way of Chuang Tzu. Wu graciously informed Merton that his grasp of Chinese philosophy was far from superficial. Wu also had done his homework! Referring to an article he had read by Merton on classical Chinese thought, he reassured the monk of Gethsemani, "There is absolutely nothing 'superficial' about your grasp of the Confucian classics." He then added, "Your God-given gift for seeing the essentials in everything you study prevents you from in any way being superficial."[24]

Merton and Wu had affirmed each other in ways that were genuine, forthright, and knowledgeable. In neither letter can we detect any trace of paternalism. Each respected the other and tried to *awaken response* in the other, rather than gain *control* over the situation.

Each sensed, from the beginning of their correspondence, that they had met a kindred spirit; perhaps this was even truer for Wu than Merton. He accepted Merton's first letter as a gift of grace. Wu wrote Merton that after picking up his initial letter at the mailroom of Seton Hall, he purposely did not open it. Instead, he took the letter with him to the chapel, and only after Mass, still on his knees, did he open it. To understand this act is to understand John Wu. He was simply being appropriately reverent. It seems Father Paul Chan had told Wu that Merton might write. Wu, on his part, anxiously anticipated this letter. He knew of Merton and had read several of his books. He considered it a great honor to receive Merton's correspondence and therefore wanted to show proper respect. He did this prayerfully, on his knees, in the chapel setting.

This marked the beginning of a deep friendship. Through their letters, Merton and Wu discussed Eastern and Western ways of thinking. World politics also became a critical part of their discussions. One of the letters from Merton to Wu, dated June 7, 1962, is included in Merton's *Cold War Letters* (Letter 83). On that occasion Merton expressed deep concern for the plight of the Chinese refugees that the world had virtually ignored. This was, of course, a deep source of pain and concern for the expatriated Wu.

They also wrote each other about personal matters. Merton celebrated with Wu when Wu's son Peter was ordained at Maryknoll. They commiserated together when each heard the news of the other's hospitalization. And all the while, they prayed for each other. They were, in every way, bonded together as spiritual brothers.

The ultimate focus of their letters, however, was their work together on Chuang Tzu. Both realized that Merton's project on Chuang Tzu would bring greater recognition in the West for this great Eastern sage. Wu helped Merton by providing four published translations of Chuang Tzu's works. He also personally translated passages from Chuang Tzu's writings, which Merton specifically requested. Their letters are peppered with references to Taoist ideas, especially those that Chuang Tzu represented.

John Wu knew early in their relationship that Merton was the right person for the task. He wrote to Merton: "Only a man like yourself steeped in the works of the great Christian mystics can know what Lao Tzu and Chuang Tzu were pointing at, and how utterly honest and correct they were."[25] Wu believed that a Western contemplative like Merton, with his first-class intellect and deep spirit, was in the best possible position to introduce the subtle and allusive wisdom of Chuang Tzu to the West. And he was absolutely correct.

Chuang Tzu and the Tao

The great fruit of the Merton-Wu friendship was Merton's 1965 publication of *The Way of Chuang Tzu*. This book, which Merton considered among his best and most enjoyable to write, cannot be understood or appreciated apart from John Wu's collaboration. Its very creation is difficult to imagine without reference to the spiritual friendship and intellectual insights found in the Merton-Wu correspondence. It is not surprising that Merton dedicated his book on Chuang Tzu to John C. H. Wu, "without whose encouragement I would never have dared this."

In his preface to *The Way of Chuang Tzu,* Merton refers to John Wu as his "chief abettor and accomplice" in the project. He declared for all to know that "we are in this together."[26] In every imaginable way Merton delighted in the help and advice he received from Wu. They both adored Chuang Tzu. It made no difference that his writings were over two thousand years old. They both believed his wisdom was timeless—especially in understanding the Tao. It was this spiritual truth that they wanted to convey to the grossly materialistic world of the West.

Merton had learned well the lessons of the East. He argued in *The Way of Chuang Tzu* that the ancient sage's religious philosophy had, in fact, transcended all externals such as human convention, history, and culture. As within the Western contemplative tradition, Chuang Tzu's thought centered not on the ego—either individual or collective—but on the Tao, the mysterious spiritual way of the Universe.

The Tao, as the cosmic power of being and nonbeing, is something very subtle and indirect. It is both hidden and manifest. Like water, it can be as soft as a gentle rain, or, again like water, it can be as powerful as a raging flood. Yet, in the final analysis, the Tao is neither the former nor the latter. Like God, in many forms of Western mysticism, the Tao ultimately remains name-less—the Void. But a Void filled with meaning.

In *The Way of Chuang Tzu* Merton refers to the Tao of Chuang Tzu's writing as the "Eternal Tao." For both Merton and Wu, the Eternal Tao could not be restricted to Taoist phi-losophy. Its timeless truth permeated all of ancient China. One might choose to be Taoist, Confucian, or Buddhist; however, the Tao remains constant throughout. The Tao, if it is truly the Eternal Tao, predates and postdates any particular philosophy, then or now.

For Merton, the Eternal Tao is like the God behind God found in the mysticism of Meister Eckhart. By speaking of the Eternal Tao, Merton was trying to say something he knew could not be put into words. It is the Reality in which we live, and move, and have our being. It is closer to us than we are to ourselves. How-ever, unlike traditional Western theology, its description is in terms of the natural rather than the supernatural order of things.

Merton attempted to identify the essence of Chuang Tzu's Eternal Tao by returning to the most basic of all Taoist texts—*The Tao Te Ching.* Merton writes:

> In the first chapter of the *Tao Te Ching,* Lao Tzu distinguishes between the Eternal Tao "that cannot be named," which is the nameless and unknowable source of all being, and the Tao "that can be named," which is the "Mother of all things." Con-fucians may have had access to the manifest as-pects of the Tao "that can be named," but the basis of all Chuang Tzu's critique of Ju (Confucian) phi-losophy is that it never comes near the Tao "that cannot be named," and indeed takes no account of it.[27]

Merton lamented that Western society, much like most Confucians, knows the Tao that can be named, but it "never comes near" the Tao that cannot be named. Merton hoped that awareness of Chuang Tzu's Eternal Tao might awaken a response in the West to its own spiritual longings, for it needed to recover a deeper sense of ultimate Reality.

When John Wu received from Merton the completed text of *The Way of Chuang Tzu,* he was thrilled with what Merton had accomplished. He wrote to Merton on November 19, 1965: "I have come to the conclusion that you and Chuang Tzu are one. It is Chuang Tzu himself who writes his thoughts in the English of Thomas Merton."[28]

Wu marveled at how Merton's "free interpretative readings of characteristic passages" of Chuang Tzu captured the heart of the ancient sage.[29] In an earlier letter Wu had taken issue with Merton for calling his work an interpretation "after Chuang Tzu." He protested, "You have taken him [Chuang Tzu] by the forelocks not by the tail."[30]

Merton, with Wu's help, had indeed built a significant spiritual bridge between East and West with the publication of *The Way of Chuang Tzu.* As Wu wrote to Merton on November 24, 1965:

> You are a true man of Tao just as he [Chuang Tzu]
> is. You have met in that eternal place which is no
> place and you look at each other and laugh together.
> . . . The spirit of joy is written all over the pages.[31]

John Wu and Thomas Merton also had met "in that eternal place which is no place." Perhaps this points to the greatest accomplishment of *The Way of Chuang Tzu.* John Wu and Thomas Merton, acting as signs of peace, had reconciled within their own lives the wisdom of the East and West. And in so doing, they opened the way for others to follow.

Silent Lamp

John Wu recognized in Merton an amazing ability to step out in freedom beyond old borders into new territory—to that eternal place which is no place. This is the "place" that James Finley, in his classic study of Merton, identifies in the title of his book as *Merton's Palace of Nowhere*. Merton as a Western contemplative had allowed his freedom in Christ to carry him across boundaries from West to East. Wu also knew of this spiritual freedom as he moved uninhibited from the Eastern wisdom of his Chinese forbears to the expansive truths of his Catholic faith.

The joy that both men felt with the completion of *The Way of Chuang Tzu* was seated deep within, in that place which indeed is no place, where true wisdom and faith abide. At this depth eternal truth is present for all to grasp. Chuang Tzu knew this— and so did Merton and Wu. Thanks to the ancient sage Chuang Tzu they both were once again reminded of humanity's common spiritual ground.

Merton liked to joke that his friend John Wu was certain that in "some former life" he, Thomas Merton, had been "a Chinese monk." Out of respect, Wu even gave Merton a Chinese name— Mei Teng—which literally means "silent lamp."[32] A lamp gives light—it illuminates. But what if the experience of this illumination is beyond words? What if the light is silent?

In one of his letters to Merton, Wu summed up his friend's eternal quest for this kind of light. He writes in the profound simplicity of a haiku:

> Silent lamp! Silent Lamp! I only see its radiance but
> hear not its voice! Spring beyond the world.[33]

Sometimes, in silence, all we can do is view the light and appreciate its wisdom. To speak may be to do too much. To spring beyond the world may be to do too little. In either case, Merton and Wu would smile, knowing that ultimate Truth is to be found in that place which is no place at all, eternity.

This is the initial letter from Merton to John Wu
written on March 14, 1961. Merton expresses his
respect for Dr. Wu and his desire to study Oriental
philosophy. He especially wants to learn more about
Chuang Tzu, the ancient Taoist sage, whom he had
already read and desired to write about.

March 14, 1961

My Dear Dr. Wu:

Father Paul Chan wrote to me some time ago saying that he had kindly spoken to you about a project of mine which came to his attention, through a letter I had written to Archbishop Yu Pin. So you are already acquainted with the fact that I have been for some time persuaded of the immense importance of a prudent study of Oriental philosophy by some of us in the West, particularly in the kind of perspective that guided some of the early Church Fathers in their use of Platonism, and St Thomas in his use of Aristotle.

Naturally, there is a great deal of irresponsible and rather absurd dabbling in things Oriental among certain western types, and I don't want to make myself sillier than I already am by joining their number. Besides, I am very much lacking in background, and do not even have the most elementary knowledge of the languages that might be involved.

It is very important that one in such a position should have guidance and advice from someone who is an expert in the field. I am very glad Father Chan suggested you, as I am familiar with your books and realize that you are exactly the kind of person who would be of immense help. Since Father Chan says that you have expressed a willingness to do something of the kind, I therefore write to you without too many apologies, and indeed with deep gratitude for your kindness.

Where shall I begin? The one concrete thing that Father Chan seized upon in my letter to Archbishop Yu Pin was the tentative project of a selection from Chuang Tzu which New Directions would like to publish. But this is perhaps premature. I don't know if you saw a raw attempt of mine to say something about Chinese Thought in *Jubilee*. It may have seemed articulate but I am sure you would have realized that I have only the most superficial grasp of the Confucian Classics, which is what I was mainly talking about. I do think it would be important perhaps for me to read some more and if possible discuss the Four Classics with you on the most elementary level, like any Chinese schoolboy of the old days. I would like to really get impregnated with the spirit of the Four Classics, which to my mind is perfectly compatible with Christian ethics, and then go on to what really attracts me even more, the mysticism of the early Taoists. Then after that I might be able to talk sense about Chuang Tzu and if you are still interested, we could perhaps work together on a selection, and you could do an original translation of the things we selected. I have the Legge translation here which looks suspiciously doctored to me.

I would be interested in your reaction, and would welcome any suggestions as to how to proceed and what to read now. And then, when you are free, I would like to invite you down to Gethsemani for a few days or a week. This could be made worth while materially speaking by lectures which could be arranged at neighboring colleges and Father Abbot would certainly want you to talk here. You could perhaps address my class on mystical theology on Chinese spirituality and mysticism. In a word there would be ways of covering expenses, and no doubt you might enjoy the change. We would certainly enjoy having you here as our guest. Can we discuss this further?

Meanwhile, as a token of esteem, I am sending a privately printed thing on Meng Tzu. I keep you in my prayers and beg that this project may be fruitful in the sense in which it seems to be suggested by the will of God.

Very cordially yours in Christ

Five

Holiness

The Merton–Heschel Letters

*I am happy that someone is there, like
yourself, to emphasize the mystery and
the Holiness of God.*

—MERTON TO ABRAHAM HESCHEL,
DECEMBER 17, 1960

*W*hat a relief it is to know you are not alone. In Abraham
Joshua Heschel (1907–72), Thomas Merton had
found a soul mate who shared his distress over the
loss of holiness in modern life. When Merton initiated correspondence with Heschel in the Fall of 1960, he could not help
but express his delight in discovering a kindred spirit, who, like
himself, refused to accept the sterile one-dimensionality of modernity—a world devoid of reverence for transcendence. Merton
believed modern life had abandoned the Sacred for a shallow
and potentially destructive secularism that devalued the holiness
of God and God's creation (especially us humans). This expression of holiness, Merton believed, was deeply rooted in the Bible
and needed to be recovered.

Heschel, on his part, wholeheartedly agreed with Merton. This Jewish philosopher and holy man enthusiastically wrote to Merton on October 23, 1960:

> Your letter came as a precious affirmation of what I have known for a long time: of how much there is we share in the ways of trying to sense what is given in the Word, in the things created, in the moments He continues to create, in the effort to counteract the desecration of stillness. For many good hours in reading some of your writings, I am indebted to you.[1]

Heschel knew of Merton's work, just as Merton knew of Heschel's. But now an essential new ingredient was added: they were fast becoming interfaith friends, people of the Book, joined by a fascination for the Bible as God's word to humanity.

Merton's appreciation for Abraham Heschel and his work is succinctly expressed in a letter dated January 26, 1963. He notes not only Heschel's brilliance as a scholar but also his profound grasp of biblical revelation. In part, Merton tells Heschel:

> You take exactly the kind of reflective approach that seems to me most significantly and spiritually fruitful, for after all it is not the Prophets we study but the word of God revealed in and through them.[2]

Merton applauded Heschel for not losing sight, as so many modern scholars did, of the Bible's main subject—God.

In short, Merton found in Abraham Heschel a spiritual guide into the deeper meanings of biblical holiness. The God of Abraham, Isaac, Jacob, Moses, and the prophets came alive for Merton in his reading of Heschel. He had discovered an interfaith friend, who, like himself, desired to combine, in his own

life, the biblical legacy of a personal devotion to God with a prophetic commitment to social justice and peace. For both Merton
and Heschel, true biblical holiness must include all of this. But
who exactly was Abraham Heschel, this Jewish sage and mod-
ern-day prophet?

Abraham Heschel and Holiness

When Merton first contacted Heschel, Heschel was teaching at
the Jewish Theological Seminary in New York City. In fact, from
1945 to his death in 1972, Dr. Abraham Joshua Heschel had a
long and distinguished career at this prestigious institution as
professor of Jewish ethics and mysticism. But this professorship
marked only the last phase of a dramatic life filled with danger
and great accomplishment.

Perhaps the best summary of Heschel's life is one provided by
Heschel himself. He offered a rare insight into his own self-understanding during his inaugural lecture as the Harry Emerson
Fosdick Visiting Professor at Union Theological Seminary in
1965. Twenty-five years after his arrival in America, Heschel
defined himself as a refugee—a Diaspora Jew who sought to be
responsive to God during troubling times. He placed his life within
the context of a post-Holocaust world. According to Heschel:

> I speak as a member of a congregation whose
> founder was Abraham, and the name of my rabbi is
> Moses.
>
> I speak as a person who was able to leave War-
> saw, the city in which I was born, just six weeks
> before the disaster began. My destination was New
> York, it would have been Auschwitz or Treblinka. I
> am a brand plucked from the fire, in which my
> people was burned to death. I am a brand plucked

from the fire of an altar of Satan on which millions
of human lives were exterminated to evil's greater
glory, and on which so much else was consumed:
the divine image of so many human beings, many
people's faith in the God of justice and compassion, and much of the secret and power of attach-
ment to the Bible bred and cherished in the hearts
of men for nearly two thousand years.[3]

This was the holy man of Israel whom Merton came to love
and respect—a brand plucked from the fire." Elie Wiesel,
Heschel's close friend during his New York years, has described
Heschel as "profoundly Jewish, a deep believer and sincere pacifist who wrote lyric poems in Yiddish." Wiesel recalls in his memoirs many hours spent with his dear rabbinical friend. He
remembers that they "sometimes strolled up and down Riverside
Drive discussing God, prayer, Polish Hasidism compared to Hun-
garian Hasidism, Lithuanian Yiddish folklore, and Polish Yiddish
literature." In Wiesel's words, "Heschel was a man motivated by
humanitarian and civil virtue as well as Hasidic fervor."[4]

Most important, in Wiesel's judgment, Heschel did not "con-
duct his quest for knowledge from an ivory tower." Among other
things, "he was an active opponent of the war in Vietnam."[5]
Wiesel, like so many others, was challenged by Heschel's ability
to merge his personal piety with a prophetic witness to justice.
This truly pious rabbi became a significant part of America's conscience. Wiesel notes:

Heschel was the major spokesman for Jewish
ecumenism, a Jewish friend of all the oppressed.
He was among the first to fight for Russian Jews
and—it should be noted—for American blacks. It
was he who introduced me to Martin Luther King,
Jr., whom he revered.[6]

In remarkable ways Heschel unified his "mystical theology" with his "prophetic ethics."[7] This made him a spiritual and moral magnet for many, including Merton. Here was genuine biblical holiness.

God's Search for Humanity

In his physical appearance Abraham Heschel looked every bit the prophet, like a messenger from God who had just stepped out of the pages of the Hebrew Bible. Indeed, by the time Merton and Heschel met at Gethsemani in July 1964, this biblical prophet and sage had a very distinctive physical persona. Edward Kaplan, in his brilliant book on Heschel, *Holiness in Words,* provides us with a wonderful description of the mature Heschel.

> On the level of appearance, he was recognized as the only traditional Jew (that is, with beard and skull-cap) to take radical positions in matters of moral, political, and interreligious controversy. For Christians, especially, he seemed to resemble a Hebrew prophet, picturesque with his bushy white hair, his whiskers, vehement manner, and biblical oratory. Analysis of his poetics of social action demonstrates that, beyond the media images, Heschel's appeal was not superficial. The persona felt authentic because his message conveyed substance.[8]

Merton recognized this authenticity in Heschel. Trust between these two men was almost instant.

Merton, in his correspondence with Heschel, was able to move quickly to the heart of Heschel's message, to the substantive core of his teachings. He found this core in *God in Search of Man.* Merton writes that of all Heschel's books "I think the one that really appeals to me the most of all is *God in Search of Man.*"[9] According to Edward Kaplan, this was Heschel's "Jewish theological summa."[10] Merton quickly recognized this fact.

In Heschel's main thesis he argued that the Bible's message can only be understood in its full force when God is viewed as active throughout all creation. The Bible is not primarily a story of humankind's search for God, as moderns often view it; rather, it is a narrative of "God's search for man." Merton resonated with this radical reverence, which insists that in the human and divine encounter the initiative is always God's.[11] Our search for God is by no means invalid, but we must not forget that God seeks us out long before we seek out God. This rang true to Merton's own experience.

Heschel's understanding of the Bible's essential message—God in search of humanity—had major implications for Merton's thinking. What if the word, which comes to us from the prophets, is not a human word at all? What if this word truly comes from God? This presents us with a great challenge, if taken seriously. Given all our human limitations, how can we possibly get the message right? Won't we confuse the message? Merton and Heschel would not disagree that we have a penchant for not understanding the biblical God. However, God is not deterred by this and continues to seek us out. In what can only be called an act of holiness, God's presence has entered our lives. The question is whether we will acknowledge it and respond.

How does God search us out? Does God actually speak? In a passage from *God in Search of Man,* with which Merton was very familiar, Heschel reminds his reader:

> When Adam and Eve hid from His presence, the Lord called: *Where art Thou* (Genesis 3:9). It is a call that goes out again and again. It is a still small echo of a still small voice, not uttered in words, not

> conveyed in categories of the mind, but ineffable
> and mysterious, as ineffable and mysterious as the
> glory that fills the whole world.[12]

Heschel, like Merton, was convinced that God is always present to us, albeit in mysterious and often subtle ways. Our problem, however, is that we are not present to God; we are inattentive and have lost our way.

Awareness of God, for Heschel, can only be restored by repentance. And Heschel has something very particular in mind here. He writes, "The Hebrew word for repentance, *teshuvah*, means *return*. Yet it also means *answer*."[13] *Returning* to God is our *answer* to God, our response to God's seeking us out. This kind of response in Merton's Christian understanding is similar to the idea of faith itself, trusting God enough to return to our divine source.

Heschel insists that the Creator perseveres in constant pursuit of creation—especially of humankind. In this regard Heschel argues that God not only desires a restored relationship with humanity but "needs" it. This is the very nature of the biblical God. Heschel writes, "It is as if God were unwilling to be alone, and He has chosen man to serve him." Hence, in Heschel's theological understanding, "we do not have to discover the world of faith; we only have to recover it."[14]

This theme of the "recovery" of faith is very close to Merton's experience as a monastic contemplative. In *New Seeds of Contemplation* Merton writes that faith is "the opening of an inward eye, the eye of the heart, to be filled with the presence of Divine light."[15] In other words, faith is an awakening to the "Divine light" that is already present. It is a return to what is most real but often forgotten. It is a seeing, a remembering (in Heschel's terms, the experience of *teshuvah*).

With masterful use of his adopted language, Heschel writes in beautiful English prose about the world of faith:

> It is not a *terra incognita,* an unknown land; it is a
> forgotten land, and our relation to God is a palimp-
> sest rather than a *tabula rasa.* There is no one who
> has no faith. Every one of us stood at the foot of
> Sinai and beheld the voice that proclaimed, *I am
> the Lord thy God.*[16]

This sort of powerful, spiritual reflection helped bring many Jews
and Christians back to "the foot of Sinai." Among them, was
Heschel's interfaith friend Thomas Merton.

Merton's Dilemma

Due in large part to the wisdom and friendship of Abraham
Heschel, Merton rediscovered the Jewish roots that nurtured his
Catholic faith. He knew at the deepest level of his being that he
would never be spiritually whole until he embraced within himself the great lessons that Judaism had to teach—especially to
Christianity, which so often had denigrated and persecuted the
keepers of God's original covenant.

Two thousand years of anti-Semitism within the church caused
Merton great pain. He was aware of a shared sense of responsibility for the church's persecution of Jews. However, Merton's
hopes for the end of this sin of the church were raised when,
between 1962 and 1965, the Second Vatican Council seemed
positioned to right these wrongs.

Merton, as well as Heschel, had high expectations that Vatican
II would end anti-Semitism in the church. At a minimum, they
hoped that the church would go on record against anti-Semitic
behavior and seek reconciliation. And they had reason to hope.
Under the courageous leadership of Pope John XXIII the church
was beginning to change in very significant ways. It looked like the

start of a new day, and change was certainly in the air. However, with Pope John's death in the midst of the council's proceedings, hope dimmed once again. The Vatican's bureaucracy began to slow down the council's progress in areas such as interfaith dialogue.

Nevertheless, the council did address Christian-Jewish relations and produced a preliminary document. Heschel, who acted as a Jewish adviser to the council, was guardedly optimistic about this document's initial draft. But an urgent visit by Heschel to Merton at Gethsemani on July 13, 1964, revealed that the document was in trouble; it was in danger of being drastically altered. What had begun as "a truly prophetic statement" was about to be watered down and rendered ineffective "because of the concerns of bishops in Arab countries." [17]

Heschel's response to rumored changes in the document was filled with righteous indignation and despair. The church, once again, seemed more concerned with political expediencies than theological truth. What had been hailed by church progressives as a historic statement confessing *spiritual fratricide* and *complicity* in anti-Semitism now appeared to be a return to traditional views of Jews as eschatological candidates for Christian conversion. Furthermore, the revised statement was said to anticipate the future disappearance of Judaism as it discovered its true theological fulfillment in the church.

Heschel's protest was immediate and direct. He sent a mimeographed statement to the council and to Merton. It began:

> Throughout the centuries our people have paid such a high price in suffering and martyrdom for preserving the Covenant and the legacy of holiness, faith and devotion to the sacred Jewish tradition. To this day we labor devotedly to educate our children in the way of the Torah. [18]

With this sacred mission in mind, it was totally unacceptable to
Heschel that the church might persist in its desire to abort this
original covenant. Heschel rejected any movement, especially
within the church, to make Christians out of Jews. He declared
in public and in private: "As I have repeatedly stated to leading
personalities of the Vatican, I am ready to go to Auschwitz any-
time, if faced with the alternative of conversion or death."[19]

Merton responded immediately to Heschel's agonized concern. In spiritual solidarity, he wrote Heschel on September 9,
1964, that any such thinking on the part of the Vatican brought
out his own "latent ambitions to be a true Jew under my Catholic
skin." He told Heschel, it was like "being spiritually slapped in
the face" for the council to act in this manner. Merton referred to
those who wanted to change the document in the direction of
Christian triumphalism as "these blind and complacent people
of whom I am nevertheless a 'collaborator.'"[20]

Merton joined Heschel in his anger and protest. It was outrageous to him that in this situation the church took "three steps
backward after each timid step forward." Added to his outrage
was a statement by Merton reinforcing his spiritual kinship with
Heschel: "The Psalms have said all that need be said about this
sort of thing, *and you and I both pray them.* In them we are
one, in their truth, in their silence."[21]

Merton and Heschel, because of the bond of holiness they
shared, remained very close during this time of crisis. The church,
as a religious institution, might act in ambiguous and hurtful ways
toward the synagogue, but at a deeper level Merton and Heschel
preserved their personal relationship as men of prayer. To sus-
tain interfaith friendship, individuals at times must remain in solidarity despite institutional roadblocks. This was one of those times.

In a journal entry from September 10, 1964, Merton referred
to the changes made in the Vatican II document in question as
"incredibly bad." The statement on Christian-Jewish relations, in
Merton's assessment, "has become a stuffy and pointless piece

of formalism, with the *incredibly* stupid addition that the Church is looking forward with hope to the union of Jews to herself."[22] Merton knew how insensitive and wrong this kind of statement was in relation to the Jewish community. Its arrogance and wrong-headed theology would destroy any good will between Christians and Jews that the original draft of the document had set forth.

In a more nuanced response Merton wrote a letter of concern and encouragement to Cardinal Bea, the head of the council's work on the Christian-Jewish statement. Cardinal Bea favored the original draft and needed support in stemming the tide toward conservative revision. Merton offered his prayers and expressed hope that the church would rise to the occasion. Referring to the so-called Jewish chapter of this document, Merton wrote:

> The purpose of this letter is to assure your Eminence that I and my brothers here will certainly be praying that God may see fit to grant His Church the very great favor and grace of understanding the true meaning of this opportunity for repentance and truth which is being offered her and which so many are ready to reject and refuse.[23]

Merton, like Heschel, feared that a historic opportunity for the church to repent of its anti-Semitism was being lost. He told Cardinal Bea in his letter, "I am personally convinced that the grace to truly see the Church as she is in her humility and in her splendor may perhaps not be granted to Council Fathers if they fail to take account of the anguished Synagogue." For Merton, "This is not just a matter of a gesture of magnanimity. The deepest truths are in question."[24]

These words by Merton have taken on a new meaning for me ever since the summer of 2004. Visiting the great synagogue in Rome—the oldest in the Western world—some forty years after Merton wrote Cardinal Bea, I realized that the "deepest truths"

of which Merton spoke are still unresolved. With one-third of its
membership murdered in the Holocaust, I could not help but
wonder how the congregants of this synagogue within the shad-
ows of Vatican City would have responded in 1964 to the debate
taking place nearby in the privacy of the Vatican. Much indeed
was at stake. So much more than many realized. But Heschel
and Merton sensed the gravity of the situation. A historic moment could be lost.

Merton made a specific proposal to Cardinal Bea. He tried his
best to move forward his concern for improved Jewish-Christian
relations. Merton thought this might require bringing others on
board by broadening the issue, giving it a wider context. Merton's
strategy was to gain acceptance of the original draft and its intentions by adding other issues to the document. He presented
this strategy to Cardinal Bea:

> Would it not perhaps be possible, theologically as
> well as "diplomatically," to meet the objections
> raised by those who fear to alienate Moslems. . . .
> Christians and Jews together in the Koran occupy
> a privileged position as "people of the Book" and
> as spiritual descendants of Abraham. Perhaps this
> common theological root in the promises made to
> Abraham might bear fruit in a Chapter on anti-
> Semitism oriented to peace with *all* Semites and
> then with special emphasis on the relation of the
> church and Synagogue and at least an implicit rec-
> ognition of the long-standing sin of anti-Jewish ha-
> tred among Catholics.[25]

This creative proposal on Merton's part would not have been
met with full acceptance by Heschel. What Merton called "the
long-standing sin of anti-Jewish hatred among Catholics" needed

more than "an implicit recognition." Also, the insertion of a statement of Christian-Jewish relations within the broader context of a declaration on the three Abrahamic faiths would have been viewed as yet another way of watering down a long overdue statement about the church's sin of anti-Semitism.

However, much to Merton's credit, he did view the entire matter (like Heschel) as a theological issue. It cut to the heart of the church's self-identity as a people of God. Political solutions were not sufficient. As Merton noted, the council's apparent impasse on the Jewish chapter was a clear sign of the church "forgetting her own true identity."[26] Church and synagogue, Christians and Jews, were inextricably related to one another by the biblical God. Each is a covenant people. One cannot be subsumed by the other. Christians had no right to convert Jews. This was not, and should not be, a part of the church's mission.

It is difficult to measure the influence Heschel and Merton had on the eventual outcome of the council's statement on Christian-Jewish relations. But their concerns, along with those of other progressives, made an impact. Brenda Fitch Fairaday reports the surprising results of Council deliberations: "Bea moved through the Fourth session the final draft which had restored most, if not all, of the words that Heschel had spoken well of."[27]

Nostra Aetate (Declaration on the Relationship of the Church to Non-Christian Religions), which included the chapter on Christian-Jewish relations, was approved by a vote of 2,221 to 88. Fairday notes this was "a stunning victory for this, the shortest, but possibly the most influential document of the Second Vatican Council." Theological prejudices had been addressed. Anti-Semitism was renounced. The church had opened the door to future interreligious dialogue between Christians and Jews. But as Fairday cautions, "Political hindrances remain, always set to clog the wheels."[28] Merton and Heschel knew this all too well.

A Sacred Trust

Having weathered the political and ecclesiastical battles of the Second Vatican Council, the spiritual friendship of Merton and Heschel continued to deepen as their witness to the holiness of God and the dignity of humanity grew in ever-expanding circles of ecumenical involvement and work for social justice and peace. But perhaps the ultimate sign of their interfaith kinship was an invitation from Heschel to Merton to write the introduction for a Time-Life edition of the Bible. No greater compliment could have been paid Merton by his interfaith friend.[29]

Heschel entrusted to Merton the honor of introducing the Bible to a new, popular readership. Merton at first expressed reservations about "big fancy projects organized for mass-media."[30] However, in a letter from Heschel to Merton, dated December 15, 1966, Heschel told his friend, "I have consented to serve as consultant [for the Time-Life project on the Bible] because I believe that the work will be carried out with dignity and should help a great many people to find access to the Bible."[31] That was all Merton needed to hear. If Heschel endorsed the project, then Merton would put aside any qualms he might have and participate.

Echoing Heschel's own insistence that the Bible be understood as God's word to humanity, Merton wrote an introduction that could have been written by Heschel himself. He pointed to the centrality of holiness in the Bible's view of God. Indeed, God is a holy God, all of sacred scripture attests to this truth. This Reality, however, presents a real challenge to a self-centered humanity. The Bible's word is not easily embraced. Merton writes in his introduction:

> To accept the Bible in its *wholeness* is not easy.
> We are much more inclined to narrow it down to a
> one-track interpretation which actually embraces

only a very limited aspect of it. And we dignify that one-track view with the term "faith."[32]

Merton and Heschel knew that any one-track interpretation of the Bible diminished God's holiness. Such reductionism ended in a truncated faith—a kind of faith far removed from trust in the biblical God. Merton said of this one-track faith:

> Actually, it is the opposite of faith: it is an escape from the mature responsibility of faith which plunges into the many-dimensional, the paradoxical, the conflicting elements of the Bible as well as those of life itself, and finds its unity not by excluding all it does not understand but by *embracing* and *accepting* things in their often disconcerting reality.[33]

Such thoughts are quintessential Merton—and Heschel. Mature responsible faith (trust) in God is multidimensional, paradoxical, filled with conflicting elements, and all encompassing.

Indeed, a holy God draws us into a life of mystery and adventure. Reality is turned upside down. And this returns us to the persistent theme of our chapter. The God whom we thought we were seeking is actually pursuing us. Of this Merton and Heschel were certain. The Almighty calls out our name. The One whose name is too sacred to utter actually knows each one of our names.

Thomas Merton and Abraham Heschel knew and loved God in a way few others have. They lived in biblical holiness. They struggled, and they strained on tiptoes to see God—the God of biblical revelation. In so doing, they accepted life as the mystery that it is. They accepted a holiness in life that is boundless. These two interfaith friends invited others into this holiness, into a world encompassed by the love of a holy God. Long after the earthly end of these two holy men, the Reality remains. A holy God still seeks us out.

At the beginning of their correspondence on De-
cember 17, 1960, Merton wrote Abraham Heschel
telling of his pleasure in having received Heschel's
recent letter and the package of books which ac-
companied it. Merton's letter is both personal and
theologically reflective. He wastes little time in
engaging his interfaith friend in substantive dia-
logue. He makes the observation that both their
lives are "short of time" for letter writing. This rela-
tively brief letter communicates a deep sense of
spiritual kinship.

Dec. 17, 1960

Dear Dr. Heschel:

It was a real pleasure for me to get your good letter of October 23rd and the package of books, which are to me full of very
satisfying intuitions and statements. It is an added satisfaction to
have these books here at hand and to be able to meditate on
them in a leisurely fashion, instead of rushing to get them back
to the library.

I think the one that really appeals to me the most of all is *God
in Search of Man.* I do not mean that I think it contains all your
best and deepest thought, but it is what most appeals to me, at
least now, because it has most to say about prayer. This is what
I can agree with you on, in the deepest possible way. It is something beyond the intellect and beyond reflection. I am happy that
someone is there, like yourself, to emphasize the mystery and
the Holiness of God.

There are so many voices heard today asserting that one should
"have religion" or "believe" but all they mean is that one should
associate himself, "sign up" with some religious group. Stand up

Photo by Jacob Teshima

Abraham Heschel

and be counted. As if religion were somehow primarily a matter of gregariousness. Alas, we have too much gregariousness of the wrong kind, and with results that do not need to be recalled. The gregariousness even of some believers is a huddling together *against* God rather than adoration of His true transcendent holiness.

Needless to say I look forward eagerly to your book on the prophets. This fall I went through Amos carefully with my novices. It is a frightening accusation of our own age, with its prosperity, its arrogance and its unbelief. And its poverty, its injustice and its oppression. And now we are in the season when, in our liturgy, Isaiah is read daily: a season of longing for the fulfillment of divine promises, those promises which are so infinitely *serious,* and which are taken so lightly. Nor are these expectations fulfilled, for Christians, at Christmas merely. That too is another expectation. I believe humbly that Christians and Jews ought to realize together something of the same urgency of expectation and desire, even though there is a radically different theological dimension to their hopes. They remain the same hopes with altered perspectives. It does not seem to me that this is ever emphasized.

I want to send you some books of mine, and will begin with those I am certain you do not have: ones published here or by small publishers, unknown. I asked Farrar Straus and Cudahy to be sure and send you a press copy of *Disputed Questions* and I presume they have done so. You shall also receive the one being published shortly by New Directions.

The monastery is near Louisville. We are about fifty miles south of it, fifteen miles beyond Bardstown. If you ever come down to Louisville, Cincinnati, or Lexington you are close to the monastery. I do not know if you would be likely to come down to lecture at Hebrew Union Seminary in Cincinnati: if so that would be a fine opportunity to get down here. But in any case I do hope you will take seriously the thought of coming to see me some day. You are always welcome at the monastery. Meanwhile, any letter from you is a joy to me, though I realize we are both short of time and deprived of secretarial help. This accounts for my bad typing.

With every good wish, Very cordially yours

Six

Zen

The Merton–Suzuki Letters

*I will not be so foolish as to pretend to
you that I understand Zen. To be frank,
I hardly understand Christianity.*
—MERTON TO D. T. SUZUKI,
MARCH 12, 1959

*I*t has often been said that D. T. Suzuki (1870–1966) made
Zen an English word. Certainly, no one has done more to
introduce the West to Zen than this Japanese Buddhist
scholar and sage. Merton himself had been involved in a serious
study of Zen since the summer of 1956.[1] But he needed help.
And although many fine interpreters of Zen are available today
in the West, such was not the case in Merton's day. Who better
to turn to than Suzuki?

The specific occasion for Merton's initial letter to Suzuki was
an invitation to write a preface to Merton's book on the desert
fathers. Merton found many of the stories of these ancient mystics of Christian tradition to be very Zen-like. He hoped that Suzuki
would also see significant connections. From the start of their

relationship there was a clear desire on Merton's part to open a broader and deeper dialogue regarding Christianity and the Zen approach to living.

Referring to his life as a monk and a Christian, Merton wrote in his first letter to Suzuki, on March 12, 1959, "I have my own way to walk."[2] Yet that way was becoming more and more influenced by Zen. He stressed the impact Zen was having on his spiritual life:

> I have my own way to walk, and for some reason
> or other Zen is right in the middle of it wherever I
> go. So there it is, with all its beautiful purposeless-
> ness, and it has become very familiar to me though
> I do not know "what it is." Or even if it is an "it."[3]

What came next in Merton's introductory comments to Suzuki about himself must have intrigued the Japanese sage—as it does many of Merton's readers today:

> Not to be foolish and multiply words, I'll say simply
> that it seems to me that Zen is the very atmosphere
> of the Gospels, and the Gospels are bursting with
> it. It is the proper climate for any monk, no matter
> what kind of monk he may be.[4]

Could it be said that Merton himself was "bursting" with Zen although, as he confessed to Suzuki, he was not quite sure what Zen is?

Our task in this chapter is to pursue the allusive meaning of Zen as understood by both Merton and Suzuki. Their dialogue about Zen, as we shall see, is really an in-depth conversation about life itself, for Zen is no more and no less than that. Merton and Suzuki found common ground in their interfaith friendship through their experience of Zen.

D. T. Suzuki, the Zen–Man

On March 31, 1959, Suzuki responded to Merton's initial letter. "Reverend Father Merton," he politely wrote, "Thank you for your letter of March 12 which interests me very much."[5] The dialogue seemed fully engaged from the start. Suzuki sensed immediately the possibility of a lasting friendship. In fact, each realized he could learn much from the other.

But who was this Zen-man D. T. Suzuki? Who was he beyond his recognition as an interpreter of Zen to the West? By the time Merton had initiated correspondence, this venerated Japanese scholar of religion had already lived a rich and full life. As a lay Buddhist, an author, and an international lecturer, Suzuki was known in both the East and the West for his masterful expositions on Mahayana Buddhism, especially in its Zen form. Indeed, this wise old sage was a spiritual living treasure. Although there has been scholarly debate about Suzuki's precise manner of interpreting Japanese Zen to Westerners, none can fault his pioneering efforts to give voice to a Zen-like view of reality for broader readerships—East and West.

Of the many things Suzuki has said about Zen, perhaps his words from *An Introduction to Zen Buddhism* are most helpful for our discussion. According to Suzuki, "When a Zen master was once asked what Zen was, he replied, 'Your everyday thought.'"[6] Suzuki helped the world understand, especially the West, that Zen has nothing to do with a sectarian spirit. It cannot, for example, be confined to Buddhism or any other religion. It concerns itself with everyone's daily thoughts. It involves as Buddhists might say, "right mindfulness."

Suzuki stressed the universal nature of Zen:

> Christians as well as Buddhists can practice Zen
> just as big fish and little fish are both contentedly

> living in the same ocean. Zen is the ocean, Zen is
> the air, Zen is the mountain, Zen is thunder and
> lightning, the spring flower, summer heat, and win-
> ter snow; nay more than that, Zen is the man.[7]

From the beginning of their correspondence Suzuki must have
sensed that Merton was "catching on" to Zen.

Like Suzuki, Merton had grasped Zen's universality—Zen and
the Gospels viewed together. On the most personal of levels,
Merton wrote to Suzuki: "If I could not breathe Zen I would probably die of spiritual asphyxiation. But I still don't know what it is.
No matter. I don't know what the air is either."[8] This statement is
similar to Suzuki's observation that "Zen *is* the air." For all his
alleged puzzlement, Merton was closer to the truth of Zen than
he sometimes let on. Of course, Suzuki sensed this.

Born on October 18, 1870, in Kanazawa in north central
Japan, D. T. Suzuki was to spend the majority of his long life
traveling in Asia, Europe, and North America. Known to the
Western world as D. T. Suzuki, Suzuki Daisetsu Teitaro remained
true to his Japanese roots while bridging the great divide between East and West.

The youngest of five children, he attended local schools in
Kanazawa until the age of seventeen, when the money ran out.
He then taught English in nearby primary schools for several
years before moving to Tokyo in 1891 to attend Waseda University.[9] During this period of his life, the young Suzuki began to
visit the Engakuzi, a Zen monastery in Kamakura. His relationship with the abbot, Shaku Sōyen, changed Suzuki's life forever.
The abbot provided a stable foundation for the youthful scholar's
understanding of Zen. Zen soon became an integral dimension
of Suzuki's thinking. When the abbot, who attended the World's
Parliament of Religions in Chicago in 1893, arranged for Suzuki
to be an assistant to Illinois industrialist and amateur Orientalist

Paul Carus, he was more than ready. He worked as a translator and interpreter of Asian religious and philosophical texts for Carus—all the while continuing to cultivate his love for Zen.[10]

It was during the next decade that Suzuki's vocation in life was to take clear shape. He became an intellectual and spiritual mediator between Japan and the West. In America he made his first of many English translations of Buddhist texts and published *Outlines of Mahayana Buddhism* (1907) with Lazac and Company, London.

Outlines was Suzuki's core statement on the wisdom of Buddhism and was deeply influenced by his Zen perspective. It was a portent of things to come. Already in this volume Suzuki's Zen-like universal philosophy was evident. Merton, who later became familiar with this work, resonated with many of its insights. Suzuki writes in *Outlines:*

> The ever-increasing tendency of humanity to widen and facilitate communication in every possible way is a phenomenon illustrative of the intrinsic oneness of human souls. Isolation kills, for it is another name for death. Every soul that lives and grows deserves to embrace others, to be in communion . . . to expand infinitely so that all individual souls are brought together and united in one soul.[11]

This kind of outlook matched the interfaith spirit Merton sought in those who, like himself, desired to unite in themselves and to experience in their own lives "all that is best and most true in the numerous spiritual traditions."[12]

Suzuki lived and breathed Zen's universal spirit. It was a spirit of freedom, not bound by any external authority. In *An Introduction to Zen Buddhism* Suzuki explains what he considers to be the basic idea of Zen.

> The basic idea of Zen is to come in touch with the
> inner workings of our being, and to do this in the
> most direct way possible, without resorting to any-
> thing external or superadded. Therefore, Zen re-
> jects anything that has the semblance of an external
> authority. Absolute faith is placed in a man's own
> inner being. For whatever authority there is in Zen,
> all comes from within. This is true in the strictest
> sense of the word.[13]

This total awareness (satori) of one's "own inner being" (for
Merton, one's true self) was for Suzuki the only way to come fully
alive. Suzuki's rejection of any external source of authority meant
that we must assume complete responsibility for our lives and
our actions. This requires great discipline of mind and spirit, but
its result is true freedom.

Suzuki was indeed a free individual. He was not restrained by
the limits of culture or customs. In 1911 he married an American, Beatrice Erskine Lane, who, until her death in 1939, co-
edited many of Suzuki's works. The sense of freedom Suzuki
found in Zen also permitted him to develop relationships with
colleagues around the world. The chair in Buddhist philosophy
at Otani University, accepted by Suzuki in 1921 and held until
his retirement, never curbed his freedom. Otani encouraged his
engagement with the world. Generally respected for his free expression of Zen in Japan, he continued to teach Zen during the
decades of nationalistic devotion to Shintoism prior to World
War II. He published widely in Japanese, and this resulted eventually in thirty-two volumes of his collected works.[14]

However, as we have seen, Suzuki's influence was not confined to Japan. He taught and published in the West as well.
Perhaps it was his inner freedom that made him at home any-
where in the world. He traveled often to Europe, China, Korea,

and America. Although Suzuki resided in Japan until 1950, he eventually moved to New York City at the age of eighty. Under the sponsorship of the Rockefeller Foundation he lectured on Buddhism and Zen at numerous American universities. He was to hold public lectures at Columbia University for nearly a decade.

Most important, the apparent unrestrained freedom of Suzuki—the Zen-man—made him appealing to many Western intellectuals. This spiritual freedom was contagious and infected many. Others wanted to know what lessons about life Suzuki might have to teach them. These people included C. G. Jung, Karen Horney, Eric Fromm, Martin Heidegger, and of course, Thomas Merton. D. T. Suzuki died in Tokyo on July 12, 1966.[15]

The Merton–Suzuki Letters (1959–66)

Mutual interests were a hallmark of the Merton-Suzuki correspondence. In his second letter to Suzuki, Merton expressed delight that Suzuki was "indeed interested in the Zen-like sayings of the Desert Fathers."[16] He reported that he was sending Suzuki his manuscript on the desert fathers to be published in 1960 as *The Wisdom of the Desert.* Suzuki agreed to write an introduction to Merton's proposed book, and this project of interfaith cooperation seemed well on its way. However, Merton's censors from his monastic order "frowned" on the idea of an introduction to Merton's work on the desert fathers being written by a Buddhist.[17] Indeed, it was forbidden. Nevertheless, the two were able to collaborate on a dialogue that appeared in the *New Directions Annual* in 1961. By 1969, when this dialogue reappeared in Merton's *Zen and the Birds of Appetite,* the Second Vatican Council (1962–65) had cleared away the earlier barriers to interfaith publication.

Merton, from the beginning of their correspondence, was fascinated by Suzuki's ability (in freedom) to move past external differences to find intellectual common ground among the world's great religions. He admired Suzuki's spiritual acuity:

> It is certainly a matter of very great significance that Dr. Suzuki should choose, as the best and most obvious common ground for a dialogue between East and West, not the exterior surface of the Desert spirituality (with its ascetic practices and its meditative solitude) but the most primitive and most archetypal of all Judaeo-Christian spirituality: the narrative of the Creation and Fall of man in the Book of Genesis.[18]

Merton knew from experience that those anxious to defend their own religious positions would have great difficulties getting beyond "the exterior surface" in interfaith encounters. But not so with Suzuki. He, like Merton, understood that the true meeting place for interfaith encounters was in the depth of religious experience, not in religious doctrine. Thus, Suzuki was interested in the *story* of the creation and the fall, not in *doctrinal formulations*. He found something very human in the Genesis narrative.

In his second and third letters to Suzuki, Merton also focused on the human condition as expressed in Christianity and Zen. For Merton, the Christian gospel and Zen desired to know and to experience things as they truly are, to overcome all illusion—not to see a different world, but to see the world differently. For Merton, the gospel and Zen had this common effect upon people. Both jolted them out of their routine way of viewing life and challenged conventional wisdom. Merton had learned from Suzuki that Zen, like the Christian gospel, calls people back to their true selves. Self-deception and false constructs of reality are rejected.

Later Merton was to write, "The chief characteristic of Zen is that it rejects all these systematic elaborations [religious and philosophical systems] in order to get back, as far as possible, to the pure unarticulated and unexplained ground of direct experience. The direct experience of what? Life itself."[19]

Merton, in his letter of April 11, 1959, explains to Suzuki that for Christians "direct experience" involves being "in Christ." Merton affirms the "profoundly true intuitions on Christianity" Suzuki had expressed in his first letter. "I wish I could tell you," writes Merton, "with what joy and understanding I respond to them."[20] The Zen scholar D. T. Suzuki had intuitively identified the experiential nature of a life "in Christ" that Christianity professes. In brief, the gospels are about a certain kind of experience before they are about a certain kind of teaching or doctrine. The same was certainly true for Zen.

Merton realized that his Zen Buddhist friend saw Christianity, in its essence, more clearly than many Christians. He told Suzuki, "We have very much the same views, and take the same standpoint, which is, it seems to me, so truly that of the New Testament."[21] This does not mean that Merton and Suzuki agreed upon where these "same views" might lead. They did not. But a Zen-like commitment to "direct experience," unmediated by preconceived structures, did help Merton to see the gospel in new and exciting ways. He wrote to Suzuki, "The Christ we seek is within us, in our inmost self, *is* our inmost self, and yet infinitely transcends ourselves."[22] Suzuki would have agreed with all but the end of this sentence. And Merton knew and accepted such differences. The spiritual kinship remained. For Suzuki, there could be no transcendent reality, at least not in the Christian sense of a belief in God.

Merton's reading of Suzuki's writings on Zen (and his familiarity with John Wu's work) reinforced his deep-seated Christian conviction that individuals must leave behind their ego-consciousness if they are to advance spiritually. This point held true for both the gospel and Zen—with or without transcendence. The ego-self must vanish and make way for the more authentic self. This emptying of ego must occur in order to prepare the way for transformation, for new life.

This kind of transformation is never an easy process, according to Merton. So much of what he knew about himself, he wrote Suzuki, relied upon false realities created by his own ego. For Merton, this was not only a psychological predicament; at heart, it was a spiritual crisis. Thus, he wrote to Suzuki:

> You see, that is the trouble with the Christian world. It is not dominated by Christ (which would be perfect freedom), it is enslaved by images and ideas of Christ that are creations and projections of men and stand in the way of God's freedom. But Christ himself is in us as unknown and unseen.[23]

This is the Christ whom Merton sees and experiences (sometimes in Zen-like ways). He knew Suzuki would get his meaning, even while others often missed the point. Speaking of Christ, Merton wrote to his Zen Buddhist friend:

> We follow Him, we find Him . . . and then He must vanish and we must go along without Him at our side. Why? Because He is even closer than that. He is ourself.[24]

Merton concluded this section of his letter to Suzuki by expressing a feeling of deep spiritual kinship, "Oh my dear Dr. Suzuki I know you will understand this so well, and so many people do not, even though they are 'doctors of Israel.'"[25] They might not find agreement on transcendence, but they both shared in the experience of profound inwardness.

Merton, from his vantage point as a contemplative Christian monk, saw a connection between the kenotic (emptying) experience of the Christian as related to Christ, and the experience of *sunyata* (the void, or emptiness) as related to the Zen Buddhist. This is not to say Merton or Suzuki was prepared to equate these experiences. Certainly, from Suzuki's Zen perspective, the kenosis in Christian thought was headed in the right direction. However, his Zen viewpoint would ultimately have required that the Christian finally let go of the kenotic Christ (God emptying himself for the sake of the world). The result would be no God at all—literally and figuratively no holy One. But Merton could not cut that cord. The empty One was not to be dissolved but resurrected.

Merton rightly observed in *Zen and the Birds of Appetite* that the point of God, either negatively or positively expressed, is beside the point for Zen. "Zen is not concerned with God in the way Christianity is," writes Merton, "though one is entitled to discover sophisticated analogies between the Zen experience of the Void *(sunyata)* and the experience of God in the 'awakening' of apophatic Christian mysticism."[26] The value of Zen, for Merton, is its unrelenting challenge to the unexamined life. What it might have to say to theology, to our understanding of God, needed further exploration. At times, Merton did seem to get carried away in speculation (like his comparisons of desert fathers to Zen masters, or his musings about kenosis and *sunyata*), but the wise, old Japanese sage would slow him down.

For example, in response to Merton's second and third letters, which were filled with passages comparing Christianity and Zen, Suzuki gently counseled caution. "Dear Reverend Father Merton," he wrote on November 22, 1959, "Thank you very much for your sympathetic and illuminating letters, including your long supplementary paper."[27] However, with this word of gratitude came a reminder that some things cannot be rushed. Sometimes differences must simply be recognized. In Suzuki's words:

As you say, one's "intellectual antecedents" are
bound to condition everything one desires to eluci-
date in either Christianity or Buddhism. As human
beings we perhaps cannot avoid being so condi-
tioned. Some may say "historical" or "psychological" instead of "intellectual." Just the same, either
way, *we are destined to differ. The only thing we
can do in these circumstances is to be tolerant
toward each other.*[28]

Suzuki, always the diplomat, closes his letter with a thought about
the next step in their relationship. "I wonder," pondered the Zen
master, "if I shall have a chance to meet you personally."[29] These
two friends who were "destined to differ" nonetheless remained
in one spirit.

The Meeting

It would be five years before Suzuki's wish to meet Merton became a reality. In June of 1964 the Zen-man and the Christian
monk met for their one and only time in New York City. According to William H. Shannon's account, Merton "was much impressed by this Zen scholar, who soon was to be ninety-four years
of age." Merton wrote in his journal upon having met Suzuki,
"How impressive and what a warm and charming visit today!"[30]
The meeting was the result of Suzuki's initiative. On June 1,
1964, his secretary, Mihoko Okamura, sent the following greeting to Merton:

Dear Father Merton,
    Dr. Suzuki has asked me to inform you that he
will be coming to New York, arriving June 6th and

staying on until about June 24th. He wishes me to say that if he were younger he would make a journey to Kentucky to pay you a visit, but that may not be possible in this life. He wonders, however, if there is any chance of your visiting New York about that time? It would make him extremely happy to have the opportunity to meet you.[31]

Merton was uncertain if the abbot would give him permission for the trip, especially since he was spending increased amounts of time at his hermitage, which he entered completely one year later. However, much to Merton's surprise he was given permission to fly to New York. Hence, he flew by jet for the first time and arrived in late June 1964 at Kennedy International Airport for his historic meeting with Suzuki.

Merton and Suzuki visited twice, having "two long talks." Merton described the old Zen-man as "bent, slow, deaf, but lively and very responsive." He records in his journal that he and Suzuki shared in the traditional tea ceremony—a very Zen-like thing to do. "Mihoko made the green tea and whisked it up in the dark brown bowl and I drank it in three and a half sips as prescribed: but found it wonderful. (J. Laughlin had said it was awful.)"[32]

The talks were "very pleasant," as described by Merton, and not at all superficial. As in their correspondence and writing projects, they made critical observations about writers and current social issues. Interestingly, both agreed that they should "steer clear of movements" that promoted Zen or anything else. They shared stories and confirmed deep spiritual connections.

In a most revealing statement in his journal, Merton summarized the whole experience, "For once in a long time I felt as if I had spent a moment in my own family."[33] Mihoko Okamura and Suzuki had made Merton feel welcome and at home—at home in a New York City hotel room! Perhaps, this is the most important meaning of Zen, that is, to be fully present, to be completely alive, to be finally at home in the world.

In a tribute Merton wrote shortly after Suzuki's death in 1966, he recalled their "unforgettable" meeting. According to Merton, the last words Suzuki said in their final meeting before the usual goodbyes were "The most important thing is Love."[34] Merton was deeply moved by these words. In the end, that is what Zen and Christianity and life are all about. Thomas Merton and D. T. Suzuki knew and experienced this truth deep within their Zen-like hearts.

In this introductory letter written to D. T. Suzuki by Merton on March 12, 1959, Merton initiates a very important interfaith friendship. Merton's interest in Zen, and what he perceived to be the Zen-like quality of the desert fathers, prompted him to explore whether Suzuki saw the kind of spiritual connection he did. Of course, like many of Merton's letters, there are numerous topics in play. The complete unedited text of this March 12, 1959, letter provides an excellent example of Merton's active mind and expanding spirit.

March 12, 1959

My Dear Dr. Suzuki:

Perhaps you are accustomed to receiving letters from strangers. I hope so, because I do not wish to disturb you with a bad-mannered intrusion. I hope a word of explanation will reconcile you to the disturbance, if it is one.

The one who writes to you is a monk, a Christian and so-called "contemplative" of a rather strict Order. A monk, also, who has tried to write some books about the contemplative life and who, for better or worse, has a great love of and interest in Zen.

I will not be so foolish as to pretend to you that I understand Zen. To be frank, I hardly understand Christianity. And I often feel that those who think they know all about the teachings of Christ and of His Church are not as close to the target as they think. And I think, too, that many of the Americans who are excited about Zen are perhaps dealing with something in their own imagination, and not with a reality. It is not my business to make judgements about any of these people.

COURTESY OF THOMAS MERTON CENTER

Thomas Merton with D. T. Suzuki,
meeting in New York in June 1964

All I know is that when I read your books—and I have read
many of them—and above all when I read English versions of the
little verses in which the Zen Masters point their finger to something which flashed out at the time, I feel a profound and intimate agreement. Time after time, as I read your pages, something
in me says "That's it!" Don't ask me what. I have no desire to
explain it to anybody, or to justify it to anybody, or to analyze it
for myself. I have my own way to walk and for some reason or
other Zen is right in the middle of it wherever I go. So there it is,
with all its beautiful, purposelessness, and it has become very
familiar to me though I do not know "what it is." Or even if it is
an "it." Not to be foolish and multiply words, I'll say simply that
it seems to me that Zen is the very atmosphere of the Gospels,
and the Gospels are bursting with it. It is the proper climate for

any monk, no matter what kind of monk he may be. If I could not breathe Zen I would probably die of spiritual asphyxiation. But I still don't know what it is. No matter. I don't know what the air is either.

The purpose of this letter is not merely to thank you for your books, or to say that I am eager to read the results of your conversations with my friend Erich Fromm, another matter to ask of you.

Enclosed with this letter are a couple of pages of quotations from a little book of translations I have made. These are translations from the hermits who lived in the Egyptian Deserts in the 4th and 5th centuries A.D. I feel very strongly that you will like them for a kind of "Zen" quality they have about them. If you agree that they are interesting and that they show this particular quality, I wonder if you would let me send you the complete manuscript, which is quite short, and if you would do me the very, very great honor of writing a few words of introduction to it. The book will be published by one of two well known New York houses, in this definitive edition (though at present a limited edition is being hand printed by a friend of mine, without a preface). I cannot assure you too strongly of my conviction that a preface from you would be a great and estimable favor. To be plain, I can think of no one more appropriate for the task, because in all simplicity I believe that you are the one man, of all modern writers, who bears some real resemblance to the Desert Fathers who wrote these little lines or rather spoke them. I feel therefore that the task belongs to you by right, and that the Desert Fathers themselves would want no one else to do it. I do hope you will be able to say "yes" to this clumsy request of mine.

Whether or not you can do this, I hope at least you will let me know the address of some publisher in Japan or else where where I might be able to get some unusual Zen texts that are not easily available in the U.S.

I have been rather fortunate in getting at some of the books available here and know the work of Alan Watts, including a recent book with a good bibliography. I have borrowed your books from libraries and have only two here, the American paperback collection and the Studies in Zen put out in London. I think I can keep track of the volumes published by Rider as they come out.

Are you coming back to America? Would there ever be a chance of your passing through Kentucky and visiting our monastery? Our Father Abbot has granted me permission to see you and speak with you should you happen to come here, and it would be to me a most wonderful pleasure to do so. We are quite near Louisville. I am sure that a lecture by you could be arranged at one of the nearby Universities to make it plausible for you to come to this out of the way place.

Or perhaps you have some friend in America who understands all these things and would be interested. He has only to let me know, and perhaps something could be arranged.

Now I have taken much of your time. I hope you will find something congenial in these few little quotations and that you will be interested in my proposal. Meanwhile I close with every good wish and every desire that you be filled with all spiritual blessings—and with the hope that we may commend one another to God each in his own way. I certainly will do so in mine, and may the Lord bless you in everything.

Faithfully yours in Christ

Seven

Openness

The Merton–Hinson Letters

*My own belief about my vocation is that
I should go on not only to a more solitary form of life but also to one in which
there would continue to be a certain
openness to the world. Naturally the
combination would be difficult.*

—MERTON TO GLENN HINSON,
DECEMBER 4, 1964

*a*t the very time that Thomas Merton's interfaith correspondence and friendships were flourishing, he made
his long-awaited move toward greater solitude as
Gethsemani's first hermit. This move, which was finally permitted by Abbot Dom James in 1965, allowed Merton to take up
full-time residency in his hermitage, a little less than a mile from
the monastery. This meant a life even more closed off from the
world than his previous cloistered existence at the abbey.

Yet, as Merton had written to Glenn Hinson, he desired to
maintain "a certain openness" to the world. Indeed, the world had
beaten a path to Merton's door for many years. His face-to-face

meetings with those from the outside world had been quite numerous. The almost "steady stream of persons," as described by John Eudes Bamberger, included individuals of "multifarious interest." According to this fellow monk, there were "Vietnamese Buddhists, Hindu monks, Japanese Zen-masters, Sufi mystics, professors of religion and mysticism from Jerusalem's University, French philosophers, artists and poets from Europe, South America, and the States, Arab scholars, Mexican sociologists and many others."[1] With Merton's move to the hermitage this flow of pilgrims would subside but not end completely. Some still managed to visit Merton at his hermitage (both invited and uninvited guests).[2] Although he mostly discouraged visits, it would be fair to say that Merton never fully resolved the tension between his genuine desire for solitude and his ongoing love affair with the world.

Two things are clear, however. First, the hermit's life did, for the most part, agree with Merton. He writes in his journal: "This life is what I have always hoped it would be and always sought. A life of peace, silence, purpose, meaning."[3] In the second place, he still wanted to remain open to the world. His December 4, 1964, letter to Glenn Hinson certainly confirmed this. The challenge for Merton was how to do both—to live the hermit's life of solitude and, at the same time, be in communication and solidarity with the world and its many problems. Merton was determined not to turn his back on the world as he had done when he became a Trappist so many years before.[4] This was not to be repeated. In fact, as early as 1949 Merton had begun to realize that the life he sought "with God alone" was not to be a life of splendid isolation. He wrote at that time, "The closer the contemplative is to God the closer he is to other men."[5] For Merton, this closeness to others came to mean the world outside the monastery as well as his brother monks within. A life with God alone as his focus meant, for Merton, an unconditional love for all creation—especially for other human beings.

The mature Merton had discovered that he must remain open to the world—even as a hermit. Openness, for Merton, meant both openness to God *and* openness to humanity. In fact, this represents one of the greatest lessons we can gather from Merton's life. It was a key lesson in his interfaith friendships, especially the one that developed between Merton and a young Baptist seminary professor named Glenn Hinson. Their openness to each other stimulated an expansive Catholicism in Merton and an expansive Protestantism in Hinson. The result was a growing ecumenical spirit in both men that stretched far beyond the boundaries of their own religious traditions.

Merton—the Expansive Catholic

Thomas Merton, the mature Trappist monk, and Glenn Hinson, the young Baptist professor of church history, befriended one another in 1960. This marked the first truly significant relationship Merton had with a Protestant since becoming a Trappist. Their face-to-face meetings and their correspondence represent one of Merton's earliest attempts at interfaith dialogue—in this case, a dialogue between Catholic and Protestant Christians.

Hinson first met Merton when he arranged for Protestant seminary students from Southern Baptist Theological Seminary in Louisville to visit the monastery at Gethsemani. It was Fr. Louis who met and discussed Trappist life with Hinson's seminarians. According to William H. Shannon, Merton had been "eager to enter into dialogue with others and began meeting with Protestant groups that came to visit the Abbey of Gethsemani."[6] The time was ripe for the two men to meet. Hinson too was "eager to enter into dialogue with others." In his case, of course, the "others" were Catholics.[7] Merton, for his part, wrote favorably about his meetings with Protestant seminary professors during this time (foremost among them, Glenn Hinson). In correspondence with John Harris, a friend and schoolteacher from England, Merton reported in 1960:

> One thing here [Gethsemani] is that I am having occasional meetings with good and earnest Protestant seminary professors, and we sit and talk and discover how much we really agree on many things and that if we cannot change the situation about our respective groups, we perhaps are not expected to change it. But that there are many other things we can change in ourselves. This I think can be fruitful.[8]

Merton's conviction that "there are many other things we can change in ourselves" is an important step forward in preparing for genuine dialogue. This attitude was far different from the viewpoint he had held as the young petulant monk who wrote *The Seven Storey Mountain*. The spiritual value of this classic autobiography notwithstanding, the Merton of that work was stubbornly Catholic. Indeed, his negative description of his boyhood Anglican religious instruction at Oakham is a case in point. Further, the pre–Vatican II church into which Merton was baptized was sternly set against any real association with other Christian groups. The younger Merton shared this firm position. As William H. Shannon has observed:

> The Roman Catholic Church into which Thomas Merton was baptized could hardly be called ecumenical. Basking in the certitude of its conviction that it alone was the true church of Christ, it had no inclination to engage in dialogue with other Christians. If there was any conversation at all, it was only to convince the others that they were wrong and that the only way to salvation open to them

was to accept the authority and teachings of the
one true church of Christ. Merton embraced this
mentality.[9]

However, Merton's pre–Vatican II church had no corner on
the market of ecclesiastical truimphalism. Most of the Baptist
seminarians Merton met in Glenn Hinson's group would have
held similar absolutist views about their form of Protestantism
being the only true church. They were as predisposed to reject
Catholic belief as Catholics were to dismiss theirs. As Hinson
wrote to Merton in November of 1964, "Many of them [the semi-
narians], as you have probably been aware, have come to the
Abbey with hostility."[10] There was ample religious prejudice on
both sides of this great ecclesiastical divide in Christianity.

Since we are focused here on Merton's entry into ecumenical
conversations, we would do well to remind ourselves just how
negative the younger Merton had been toward Protestantism. In
so doing, we can appreciate how far he had come in his early
ecumenism. A little more attention to this area will remind us
that the need for greater openness to others can never be taken
for granted, even in the case of a Thomas Merton.

In *The Seven Storey Mountain* Merton viewed Protestantism, at best, as an inferior expression of Christianity. In his early
days as a zealous Catholic convert he suspected that Protestants
lacked any genuine spirituality. Protestants seemed to be more
concerned about one another in their worship than about God.[11]
In reference to a Protestant spiritual director that Merton's father had arranged for him in his youth, the writer of *The Seven
Storey Mountain* could remember only that this man was "prac-
tically useless."[12]

Even the Quaker tradition, which Merton appreciated for its
contemplative use of silence, was in the final analysis considered
to be deficient. He wrote that the Quakers were, in the end,
what they claimed to be—a Society of Friends—and nothing more.

They failed the ecclesiastical test like other Protestants.[13] In sum, at every turn in *The Seven Storey Mountain* Protestants were pictured as inferior believers when compared to the spiritual depth and ecclesiastical grandeur of Merton's Catholic Church.

This, of course, was not the perspective of the mature Merton whom Glenn Hinson met in 1960. He had changed immensely. Hinson, himself a scholar of religion, has provided insightful observations about his friend's ecumenical transformation in an article entitled "Expansive Catholicism: Ecumenical Perspectives on Thomas Merton." Here Hinson notes that Merton "underwent a vast evolution from his early period as an overzealous convert to his last days as a fully formed Catholic." In fact, he claims that by the 1960s Merton "had laid hold of an expansive view of Catholicism which, in accordance with more recent trends in Protestant as well as Roman Catholic ecumenism, looked beyond the unity of Christians with one another to their unity with humankind."[14]

Hinson judged that this spiritual evolution was born of a deep, internal struggle within Merton. A movement toward greater openness toward others, especially those who are different, was a difficult but liberating experience for the Gethsemani monk. Hinson expressed his insights on this dimension of Merton's development:

> A process of maturation is clearly discernible in Merton's attitude toward other Christians, toward other religions, and toward nonbelievers. This process seems to have kept pace with or possibly a step ahead of official changes in the Roman Catholic Church's attitude. What I suspect is that he experienced a personal liberation during a period of sustained physical and emotional struggle between 1949 and 1951 and afterwards eagerly snatched at every encouragement from the church's pronouncements

> to expand his ecumenical horizons. His growing
> concerns about the future of humanity kept stretch-
> ing those horizons farther and farther as he searched
> in universal experience for answers to the gripping
> problems of Western civilization.[15]

Thomas Merton was indeed to become the expansive Catholic—
beginning in a small, but significant way with his encounter with
Protestants like Glenn Hinson.

Glenn Hinson—the Expansive Protestant

Who, in fact, was this Protestant professor that Merton met in
1960? A helpful way to identify Hinson is to see him as the flip
side of his own thesis about Merton; if Merton was the expansive
Catholic, then Hinson is the expansive Protestant. Without question, Hinson overcame his Baptist tradition's anti-Catholicism in
a manner similar to Merton's departure from the Catholic
Church's pre–Vatican II belief that it was the only true church.
    Born in St. Louis in 1931, Glenn Hinson grew up on a farm
in the Missouri Ozarks. Raised as a Baptist, Hinson was at home
in a church that stressed the importance of being Bible-believing,
born-again Christians. Personal testimony about an individual's
conversion experience was paramount. This kind of piety was
something Baptists judged to be missing in most other Christian
groups, especially in Catholics. Indeed, it was commonplace for
Baptists to consider Catholics as not being real Christians. They
lacked a personal relationship with Jesus Christ. Any church that
followed the human authority of the pope rather than the divine
word of the Bible was considered highly suspect, if not down-
right heretical.
    Hinson reports that not until his college years at Washington
University in St. Louis did he discover within himself "an interfaith

outlook in the making." His courses in religion, especially with Huston Smith, opened his eyes to how other religious traditions could enrich his own spiritual journey. He writes, "From that point on I recognized how much different faiths share, as Abraham Heschel has said, 'at the level of fear and trembling.'"[16]

The college years thus marked the beginning of Hinson's expanding Protestant outlook. His formal education served him well in this regard. After Washington University (B.A.), he went to the Southern Baptist Theological Seminary (B.D., Th.D.), and later to Oxford University (D.Phil.). His teaching career (he also was an ordained Baptist minister) spanned more than three decades at Southern Baptist Theological Seminary, which at that time was considered one of the best Baptist theological schools in America.

At Southern, Hinson cultivated his expansive Protestantism. He was broadly recognized as a pioneer in ecumenism among Baptists. In Hinson's own words:

> What was happening with the election of Pope John XXIII and meeting Merton in 1960, of course, took me quickly from a predominantly inter-Protestant ecumenism to an all-Christian ecumenism. My friendship with Merton and with Douglas Steere [the great Quaker ecumenist], who was quite avant garde in interfaith perspectives, nudged me well beyond the Christian sphere during the early 70s. Now the urgency of interfaith dialogue and action has been added to my concerns.[17]

Hinson, now in retirement, continues to live out his expansive Protestant faith. He has published nearly thirty books on topics in church history, ecumenism, spiritual formation, and peace-making. He has held numerous leadership positions within the ecumenical movement. He continues to be a member of the

Ecumenical Institute of Spirituality and has served as the general editor of the three-volume set of Doubleday Devotional Classics. He has taught and lectured in numerous colleges, universities, and seminaries around the world. Among Baptists, it would not be an exaggeration to call him Mr. Ecumenism.

However, Hinson's journey to an expansive Protestantism has been far from easy. Ironically, fellow Baptists have often attempted to block his way. In the 1980s fundamentalists within the Southern Baptist Convention gained control of his denomination (the largest Protestant denomination in the United States). Hinson quickly became a major voice of dissent from within. But there was no stopping the fundamentalist takeover. Soon seminaries like Southern, where Hinson was a leading light, fell under the control of a fundamentalist board of trustees, and professors like Hinson were asked to adhere to a narrow statement of faith. This abridgement of academic freedom was a frontal attack on the principle of religious freedom—so central to Baptist tradition and polity. And Hinson called this heretical action by name.

After a protracted struggle, Baptist ecumenist Glenn Hinson had to relocate to the Baptist Theological Seminary at Richmond, Virginia. This school had been formed to keep alive the progressive and historic Baptist spirit that had been so brutalized by Baptist fundamentalists. Hinson understood, better than most, that fundamentalists of any sort, in any religion, operate out of an atmosphere of fear rather than love. Such people and movements sought, and continue to seek, separation rather than unity, control rather than liberation.

In 1999, Glenn Hinson retired from his position as professor of spirituality and as the John F. Loftis professor of church history at the Baptist Theological Seminary in Richmond. But he continued his service to the Christian gospel as visiting professor at Lexington Theological Seminary and with teaching at Louisville Presbyterian Seminary, the Baptist Seminary in Lexington, and Bellarmine University. Always the expansive Protestant,

Hinson continues to bear witness to what is best and most true in all faiths, including his own beloved Baptist tradition.

In many ways Glenn Hinson's spiritual trajectory has been much like Merton's. Both individuals found themselves ahead of the ecumenical curve within their respective religious traditions. They both embraced more and more of the wisdom of other faiths while digging more deeply into their own. From the start, Hinson's comprehensive interest in the history of Christianity pressed and challenged fellow Baptists who tended to focus on biblical studies and "practical theology." His in-depth scholarship opened his students and readers to the expanse of historic Christianity far beyond his own free-church tradition.

In addition to his Baptist emphasis on religious freedom and peacemaking, Hinson fully embraced the rich history of Catholic spirituality. A mark of the respect he gained among Roman Catholics was his appointment as visiting professor at St. John's University in Collegeville, Minnesota, and later as visiting professor at the Catholic University of America in Washington, D.C. (in the 1980s). The very notion of a Baptist teaching spirituality to Catholics at Catholic universities is quite unusual, even in a post–Vatican II world. It will come as no surprise, then, to learn that Hinson also has served as treasurer and first vice president of the International Thomas Merton Society.

On another ecumenical front Hinson's promotion of peace and social justice joined him to many Quaker causes. Deeply influenced by Douglas Steere, he has been an integral member of the Ecumenical Institute of Spirituality, which advances inter-Christian and interreligious interaction and understanding.[18] In addition, Hinson's ever broadening ecumenical involvement led him to work with the World Council of Churches and interreligious groups like the Graymoor Ecumenical and Interreligious Institute.

In sum, Hinson is about as much a typical Baptist as Merton is a typical Trappist (if there are such things). He is a world scholar and ecumenist with competency in numerous languages (like Merton). However, he wears his mantle of scholarship with a profound spiritual sensitivity and a genuine humility (again, like Merton). It would be accurate to say that this Baptist professor and pastor, met by Merton in the early 1960s, became a truly expansive Protestant—a leading intellectual and spiritual guide among Baptists in America during the twentieth century. Glenn Hinson was, and is, another of Merton's interfaith friends who exist for the world as a sign of peace.

The Merton–Hinson Letters (1960–67)

Merton and Hinson were convivial spiritual companions from the very beginning of their relationship. It has become commonplace by now to make this sort of statement. Those who are interfaith friends—signs of peace—seem to find kinship with one another almost immediately. Hinson was impressed with Merton from the start, especially with his openness to those different from himself. In a letter sent to Merton on November 18, 1964, Hinson notes, "I personally have never met anyone who has your openness of mind and receptivity to the thoughts of others."[19] Hinson, himself, close by in Louisville, had many opportunities for visits to Gethsemani in the early 1960s. At first, however, Hinson was reluctant to visit Merton too often. He did not know of the many friends who visited Merton at Gethsemani.

Hinson has told me that initially he kept his contact with Merton to a bare minimum out of respect for Merton's cloistered vocation. But he soon learned of Merton's widespread correspondence and of the frequent visits to Gethsemani by Merton's friends from the outside world. Hinson said that after this he increased his level of interaction with Merton, while maintaining respect for the privacy of Merton's contemplative life.

Hinson also reminded me that when Merton and he first met he was a young seminary professor not yet thirty years of age. He recalls that he did not realize how significant Merton was (or would be). But that soon changed, and Hinson knew he had befriended someone truly special.[20]

In 1961, Merton responded favorably to Hinson's invitation to visit Southern Seminary. He wrote to Hinson on May 8, 1961:

> This Friday, May 12, I have some business in Louisville and I thought it might provide an opportunity for me to drop off at the Baptist Seminary, as I said I might do when you were last here. I generally get into town about 9:30 and will probably drop in your office about that time of the morning. . . .
>
> Looking forward to meeting you again, and some other faculty members perhaps.[21]

Merton had addressed this letter to "Dear Dr. Hinson" and closed "Fr. Louis Merton." This formality, however, soon changed in later correspondence to "Glenn" and "Tom." It is evident from this early letter that Merton was quite serious about venturing into ecumenical dialogue. And he intended to do it informally and without fanfare—just "drop off." This was pure Merton.

Indeed, a hallmark of this dialogue, and any ecumenical work by Merton, was his insistence on doing it on a personal level, on giving the encounter a human face. There could indeed be no substitute for this kind of personal meeting, whether through direct contact or, more often in Merton's case, through correspondence. William Shannon has made a similar observation in *The Thomas Merton Encyclopedia.* He notes:

> It is important to make clear that Merton's perspective on interreligious dialogue differs from what could be called "professional" ecumenism. Ecumenical

dialogue, as it is generally understood, is concerned
with refining doctrinal language for the purpose of
identifying points of agreement and disagreement,
with the hope, at least among Christians, of nar-
rowing differences and working toward eventual
reunion of the separate churches.[22]

As valuable as this kind of ecumenism might be, this was not
what Merton was about as he visited Baptist professors at their
seminary in Louisville. His purpose was different. Again in the
words of William Shannon:

Leaving to the "professional" ecumenists the task
of recovering a unity that had been lost because of
human frailty, weakness, and intolerance, he
[Merton] directed his search toward a unity that had
never been lost, because it is beyond the reach of
human weakness. It can be discovered only at the
level of religious experience—something that can
never be adequately expressed in doctrinal formulations.[23]

It was at this most personal level that Merton and Hinson's friendship grew.

God of Peace

From the very start of their friendship Merton and Hinson had
discussed matters of peacemaking in a nuclear-charged world.
On his first visit to Gethsemani with his seminarians, in November 1960, Hinson talked with Merton about peace. Hinson recalls that at this time Merton was "turning toward the world,"
and their discussion about the possibility of nuclear holocaust

seemed to stimulate Merton's thoughts about the entire subject of war and violence. Not long thereafter, on April 8, 1961, Merton entered his first journal comment about peace and his opposition to nuclear war.[24]

Subsequently, in a letter dated December 22, 1962, Thomas Merton encouraged Glenn Hinson to move ahead with plans to study at Oxford. Merton knew that this experience would be educationally important to the young Baptist educator and pastor. It would be an opportunity to view the world from outside the United States. He wrote to Hinson: "If you need any encouragement to go to Oxford I would add mine, except of course I tend to be prejudiced in favor of Cambridge."[25] Merton knew firsthand the value of experiencing different cultures and gaining fresh perspectives, especially in a time of nuclear brinkmanship.[26] He knew this experience would be life-changing for Hinson.

Merton recognized that something happens to our view of the world once it is seen from another's perspective. We are forced to take into account that others often do not see things the way we do. Such awareness is heightened by living outside our own cultural and political comfort zone. Something very significant also happens to our spirits—deep within—that changes us forever. Our spirit expands.

Hinson's views did change as he lived and studied at Oxford. As a pacifist, he had long been opposed to war on theological grounds—God was a God of peace and not of war. Now, Hinson was convinced on political grounds, as well as theological grounds, that his country's war in Vietnam was a travesty. His position on the war gained clarity. He wrote to Merton on September 12, 1967, that he could no longer support the United States in its destructive and violent involvement in Southeast Asia.

Hinson reported to Merton that in England and Europe he had found no support for America's actions in Vietnam. He noted European respect for the late John F. Kennedy, but none at all for Lyndon Johnson and his escalation of the Vietnam War.

Hinson also was struck by the lasting effects of the Second World War on the European psyche. He wrote to Merton, "We Americans can hardly imagine the average European's dread of war, for we have no bomb craters in our backyards."[27] Like Merton, Hinson identified most strongly with the suffering that modern warfare brought to civilian populations. Spiritually, war was a sign of our failure to remember the peaceful intent of God's original creation. As Merton wrote in September 1966: "The people who are being burned, cut to pieces, destroyed. They are the victims of both sides."[28]

Both Merton and Hinson took a prophetic stance against the war in Vietnam. They viewed Vietnam as a senseless and costly war. Many other Americans would come to this position. However, in 1966 Merton and Hinson were minority voices in their religious opposition to the war and its massive destruction of life. Baptists and Catholics in the United States were still very reluctant to criticize the war for fear of being labeled unpatriotic. Somehow to criticize government policy was seen as seditious activity: My county right or wrong.

Merton and Hinson were convinced that the Vietnam War was symptomatic of the larger issues of human survival that plagued the modern world. But Hinson, much to his dismay, found his church unwilling to address global issues in any meaningful way. The threat of nuclear war and the realities of racism and poverty were not seriously engaged. In his September 12 letter to Merton, Hinson lamented that "Southern Baptists have no platform to stand from." How can Baptists ever face these kind of real issues, asked Hinson, when they have "sidestepped the surface issues for a century?"[29] His church was simply unwilling to talk about issues of social justice and peace.

However, Hinson never gave up on his efforts as peacemaker or as an ecumenist. With the same letter he mailed Merton a copy of his first book, *The Church: Design for Survival.* In it he encouraged Southern Baptists to seek unity with other Christians—

a modest proposal that would enable Christians to work together in meeting the moral and spiritual challenges of modern life. He told Merton: "It is a modest first effort. But I pray that it may have some impact on Southern Baptists, enough to produce the maturation of progressives within our ranks."[30] He believed it was time for his denomination to take a hard look at itself. Did it exist for itself or for a suffering world?

Hinson's emphasis on Christian cooperation was his point of departure for achieving Christ's call to love God and our neighbor. The great social challenges of the day required, as they still do, that Christians work in unity. How can Christianity stand for God's peaceful kingdom if the churches themselves are hostile to one another and silent in the face of the world's needs? Hinson wrote to Merton about his ecumenical work:

> My main concern, you will see easily enough, is our [Southern Baptists'] participation in the Christian unity movement. This has to be stated rather hesitantly, though perhaps without equivocation, at this time.[31]

Hinson, in fact, never equivocated on Christian unity or peace or the need for justice. And in ever expanding circles these commitments led him to seek cooperation among all God's children, regardless of religion or creed.

Openness and unity, peace and justice; these are cut from the same cloth for Hinson. They are all part of the fabric of God's will for our creation. This Baptist professor, like his interfaith friend Thomas Merton, knew that unity rather than division was the true mission of Christ's church—whether Protestant or Catholic. Only then could peace with justice be realized inside and outside the church. Furthermore, both of these spiritual friends were prepared to expand their faith far beyond the boundaries of Christianity itself. But the first step toward any such unity must be openness to expand our vision, first within the church, and then beyond. These interfaith friends were prepared to embrace God's vision for a world without boundaries—a world in which spiritual kinship has no limitations. The God of peace requires nothing less.

Glenn Hinson at the grave of Thomas Merton

In Merton's December 4, 1964, letter to his inter-
faith friend Glenn Hinson, the tension between
Merton's desire to become a hermit and his wish to
maintain his ecumenical contacts is front and cen-
ter. The tension between being in the world as an
"ecumenical monk" and living at his hermitage may
never have been fully resolved. The letter below
gives a window through which that struggle can be
viewed.

Dec. 4, 1964

Dear Glenn:

It has been some time since I got your fine letter and I have
wanted to do some thinking and consulting before answering it,
especially the part about going on with the dialogue that has so
evidently been blessed. Of course, in an offhand remark, I was
not able to indicate what precisely is involved. And since too it is
a matter of experiment here, the issue is not altogether clear cut.
It is not something for which ready made decisions already exist.
But on the other hand it is a matter that my Abbot wants to
direct personally according to his views. I will try in a few words
to give you the picture, with its domestic intricacies.

My own belief about my vocation is that I should go on not
only to a more solitary form of life but also to one in which there
would continue to be a certain openness to the world. Naturally
the combination would be difficult. But in the present situation,
one has to advance with one step at a time. In the monastic
orders there is a sort of kairos in the air, and part of this is the
manifest opportunity to break out into a kind of desert solitude.
In other words it means a chance to recover an essential monastic dimension that has been largely lost, and also to get beyond

institutional rigidities. I am convinced that this is something very important for monks, but I do not expect everyone to agree with that. But I am quite sure that this is the moment to move in that direction. A quite unexpected turn of events and a new look on the part of higher superiors has provided an altogether surprising opportunity, and I am the only one really in a good position to take it. So, for myself and above all for the rest of the monks who have similar aspirations everywhere, I think it becomes my duty to respond to this, and take the chance of a more completely solitary life partly in order to show that it is practicable and worth while for monks today. If this should work, then it will mean the relaxing of distrust and a new openness on the part of Superiors, and it will mean an incalculable difference for some monks who really need this kind of thing. I would be inclined to say, personally that this response to one charismatic opportunity would surely lay open the way to others and in the long run I think the ecumenical dialogue would also come in for its share of the renewal, in some way that I cannot at present foresee.

I would personally think that I could combine more solitude with occasional meetings with your groups, as in the past. But the decision on this point is not mine. The Superiors are anxious for this experiment to take place in certain definite clear cut terms, and I can see their point, from the administrative angle. They want to know precisely what is involved in this hermit business. So it becomes necessary to meet their specifications, and I am left no choice in the matter. Actually, it does simplify things and make the issue more practical, from the point of view of getting the hermit life recognized once again.

The unfortunate result is that I will not be able to carry on ecumenical conversations and contacts as before, at least for some time. I will also have to cut down on some of the writing, particularly book reviews and writing for periodicals, once I have finished the back log that I have undertaken.

Eventually I will also have to drop my work in the novitiate and other teaching assignments in the monastery itself. It seems that 1965 is going to be a sort of transition year. While waiting for the move to get some kind of definite approval from the General Chapter I will be living more continuously in the hermitage while carrying on my work in the monastery, and testing out some of the uncertain areas in the experiment.

Naturally it is a real sorrow and a sacrifice for me to renounce my meetings with your students. I have felt, as you have, that our meetings were really blessed with a breath of life and openness, and I have no doubt that this is something God wants very much from us. I hope that others will be able to carry on the work adequately. I have learned very much from my contacts with my friends there at the Seminary, and I don't think I will ever be capable of returning to a narrow and rigid view of the Church any more. Definitions have to be made and we have to stand by them, but in fact we will always realize how much greater is God than anything we can explain, predict or define. His actions and His mercy in our midst always overflow our expectations, and we can never expect Him to fit in to the limits we have assigned, even when we thought He Himself was showing us where to assign them. I know that I have gained incalculably from knowing you all, and of course I am sure that we will get together again one of these days.

Meanwhile, since next year is a sort of transition year, if you remind me when Dr Whiston comes I could always ask permission to see you with him, if you could come out. Fr Abbot has only said that I must drop the meetings with groups and of course cut down individual visits, but I think there may still be room for this one. I can at least ask. He is now on the way East, but I think he would go along with the idea.

Thanks for your remarks about the drawings. I am hoping that if someone buys a few I can set the money aside as a beginning for a scholarship fund for a Negro girl student at Catherine

Spalding. If you know someone who collects pictures and is wealthy, and might be interested. . . . One or two have been sold, I understand. So evidently they were not found to be too outrageous.

With my most cordial good wishes in Christ,

Eight

Compassion

The Merton—Nhat Hanh Letters

*I suppose you are probably back in Viet-
nam by now. I thought of you today because I finished your excellent little book
on Buddhism today. It is a really good
book, and I especially liked the chapters
about contact with reality and on the
way to live the inner life.*

—MERTON TO THICH NHAT HANH,
JUNE 29, 1966

Sometimes our assumptions can be totally wrong. When
Thomas Merton wrote his interfaith friend Thich Nhat
Hanh, he thought Nhat Hanh was back in his beloved
home—Vietnam. It was the end of June 1966. Nhat Hanh had
just completed a speaking tour in the United States but was refused readmission to his homeland. He had done the unforgiv-
able; he had spoken of peace in Vietnam.

Thich Nhat Hanh was compassionate in his plea to end the
suffering of his people. Merton's own opposition to the war was
deepened and made more public as a result of his one and only

meeting with Nhat Hanh at Gethsemani in late May of that year. But these were not times of compassion. And the war raged on.

Compassion was considered unrealistic in the world of power politics and ideological confrontation. The simple, soft-spoken poet and monk of Vietnam was judged a traitor by both sides in his country's conflict. All Nhat Hanh asked was that the needless suffering of the people of Vietnam be ended. But all that the United States and China wanted was an international, ideological showdown. It was unfortunate but acceptable to the great powers that the little country of Vietnam should be the battleground. And so it was.

Compassion lost—a fatality of geopolitical conflict. Or was it? The Buddhist monk Thich Nhat Hanh and the Christian monk Thomas Merton had a different word to speak into the situation. In their interfaith friendship they spoke as one voice—the only voice that truly matters in the long run, the voice of Love, which cannot be silenced.

These monks, given more to silence than to speech, nonetheless let their voices be heard. Out of compassion for those who suffered most—those caught between warring armies—they were compelled to speak and write as witnesses for the voiceless. In doing so they shared in a remarkable friendship of interfaith solidarity, something well worth our exploration.

Teacher

The one we call Thich Nhat Hanh came to be known by his friends and students as Thay, which means teacher. Today his works have been translated into twenty-two languages and his teachings have become known worldwide. Next to the Dalai Lama, Nhat Hanh is clearly the best-known Buddhist monk and teacher at the start of the twenty-first century.[1]

Born with the name Nguyen Xuan Bao in 1926 in central Vietnam, Thich Nhat Hanh (his monastic title and name) entered the monastery of Tu Hieu at the age of sixteen. From this point forward he dedicated his life to following and teaching the way of Buddha from the perspective of the Lam Te sect of Vietnamese Buddhism. This, in fact, is the same tradition of Zen Buddhism in which D. T. Suzuki was trained (called Rinzai in Japan).[2]

Like all monks, Nhat Hanh went through a rigorous period of training during his novitiate. According to Robert H. King, the young monk, though dedicated, was often conflicted about the monastery's traditional ways of teaching:

> The most notable feature of Nhat Hanh's novitiate was the use of *gathas*, short verses designed to focus a person's mind on the activity of the moment. In the beginning Nhat Hanh was given a practice manual containing fifty of these *gathas* and told to memorize it. There was one for virtually every activity a monk might engage in during the course of a day, including washing hands and going to the toilet.[3]

This method of teaching did not please Nhat Hanh. He wondered why he must memorize so many sayings, without being given any explanation or justification for the practice. Obedience was not the issue for Nhat Hanh, and he *did* come to appreciate the Zen "sense" of the activity. Yet, he longed for a curriculum that was more expansive, more modern—a course of study that combined traditional Zen practices with an exposure to philosophy, literature, and foreign languages.[4]

While Nhat Hanh's preparation for the contemplative life, as such, was good, he did desire further education. Therefore, he and several other students moved to a small temple on the

outskirts of Saigon to study Western philosophy and science.
This placed the young monk squarely in the center of a reform
movement within Vietnamese Buddhism that had begun in the
early 1930s.

Before he was twenty-five Nhat Hanh had already published
several works and had gained a notable reputation in Vietnam as
a scholar and spiritual teacher.[5] However, Nhat Hanh insisted
that the teachings of the Buddha be brought into the public arena
of contemporary life and politics. As a reformer, he claimed it
was not enough to study only traditional texts of Buddhism. Those
committed to the dharma teachings of the Buddha must apply
them to present-day reality.

Merton agreed with this viewpoint. In *Mystics and Zen Mas-*
ters (1967) he wrote about Nhat Hanh's insistence upon reform
in Buddhism—a radical return, as it were, to a Buddhist identification with contemporary human suffering. Drawing from Nhat
Hanh's little book on Buddhism translated from Vietnamese to
French in 1965, Merton observed:

> The basic aim of Buddhism, says Nhat Hanh, arises
> out of human experience itself—the experience of
> suffering—and it seeks to provide a realistic answer
> to man's most urgent question: how to cope with
> suffering.[6]

Nhat Hanh, like Merton, based his reading of the human predicament upon experience rather than doctrine. This was the
focus of the contemplative and compassionate orientation of both
monks; neither could divorce himself from the world's current
pain and agony. Again, in *Mystics and Zen Masters,* Merton
writes:

> Anyone who heard the Vietnamese monk, poet,
> and intellectual Thich Nhat Hanh when he visited

the United States in May and June of 1966 will be
aware that Zen is not a flight from the most urgent
problems of the age. Indeed, Thich Nhat Hanh, head
of the Institute of Higher Buddhist Studies at Saigon,
and a militant in the movement for peace and for
the reconstruction of his country seems to be one
of the very few men who have anything concrete
and positive to say about the plight of Vietnam.[7]

What Merton admired so much about Nhat Hanh was his refusal to take flight from reality and his persistent application of
the Buddha's teachings to current events. As early as his first
book on Buddhism, published as a young man, Nhat Hanh had
leveled a devastating critique upon tradition-bound Buddhism in
his country. Merton's summary of his spiritual friend's critique of
traditional Buddhism was very similar to his critique of traditional
Christianity:

Traditional Buddhism, formal, rigid, doctrinaire, is
sterile, fit for the museum, irrelevant in the modern
world, not because it is out of touch with current
realities, but because it *is out of touch with human experience itself.* Once again we find ourselves on existentialist terrain, involved in a
passionate critique of that alienation which substi-
tutes ideas and forms for authentically experienced
realities. This sclerosis is of course common to all
arbitrary and purely authoritarian orthodoxies,
whether in religion, politics, culture, education, or
science.[8]

Indeed, from his earliest years as a Buddhist reformer, Nhat
Hanh had opposed "authoritarian orthodoxies" of both the religious and political kinds. Like other progressive Vietnamese

Buddhists, he had supported his country in its struggle for national independence during the French-Indochina War (1947–54). Colonialism had to be defeated. But when the corrupt national government of President Diem practiced its own form of authoritarian orthodoxy, Nhat Hanh had to oppose it as well.

In fact, by 1957 it was clear that the Diem government had decided to eliminate all political opposition. This included many Vietnamese Buddhists. Diem's family was Catholic. Some Buddhists, including Nhat Hanh, objected to Diem's heavy-handed promotion of political and religious intolerance of anyone who did not support the official government's party line. Many opponents were silenced. Many Buddhist dissenters were imprisoned, and some were killed.

The vast majority of Vietnamese Buddhists were reluctant to appear unpatriotic by publicly opposing Diem. But not so for Nhat Hanh and other young reformers—they spoke out. The journal of the All-Vietnam Buddhist Association, edited by Nhat Hanh, criticized the Diem government for its repressive policies. In *Vietnam: Lotus in a Sea of Fire* Nhat Hanh recalls, "From the moment of his assumption of power, Diem spared no effort to eliminate every form of opposition to his regime and had no faith in anyone except members of his own family and his own church."[9] The persecution of dissenting Buddhists became quite severe. In response to state violence several monks, notably Nhat Hanh's master Thich Quang Duc, immolated themselves in protest. Their self-sacrifice made international headlines.

An opportunity for national unity was lost from the start. Any unity among Buddhists themselves was forfeited when the traditional Buddhist establishment began to censor its own reformers. Nhat Hanh met increased opposition from within his own spiritual fellowship. The journal he edited was discontinued, and his teaching was criticized for its innovations.[10]

Feeling overwhelmed by "authoritarian orthodoxies" on all sides, Nhat Hanh literally retreated to the mountains outside

Saigon and, along with a few friends, established the experimental community of Phung Boi (Fragrant Palm Leaves). This was to be a place of healing, not a place of permanent retreat. It was a place for spiritual renewal so that Nhat Hanh and his friends might gain strength to return to the public arena of political conflict.

In 1966 Nhat Hanh embarked upon his first mission to the United States. He had been to America earlier to study as a student at Princeton, and then to teach at Columbia, but not as someone to speak in behalf of the Vietnamese people, who had suffered so much from the Vietnam conflict. Sponsored by The Fellowship of Reconciliation and Cornell University, he spoke with compassion and quiet dignity about the suffering of his people.

Nhat Hanh gave a human face to what many viewed as an ideological struggle between communism and democracy. He refused, on humanitarian grounds, to permit others to settle for abstractions and patriotic slogans when it was real people who suffered and died. His brief visit brought a perspective on Vietnam to the United States that had been missing. The following year Martin Luther King, Jr., nominated Nhat Hanh for the Nobel Peace Prize. He did not receive the prize, but his nomination added to his international reputation. However, in one of history's great ironies, Nhat Hanh was banned from returning to his beloved Vietnam by both the anti-Communists and later, following their victory in 1975, by the Communist government of his divided land. His peacemaking and compassion were deemed seditious by both sides.

Friend

Thich Nhat Hanh met with many influential American leaders in government and society during his 1966 trip to America, among

them Senator William Fulbright, a leading opponent of the war
in Vietnam, and Secretary of Defense Robert McNamara, one of
its staunch supporters. Characteristic of Nhat Hanh, he attempted
to speak to both sides of the conflict, offering himself as a mediator for peace and reconciliation. While in Washington he held a
major press conference and even presented a five-point proposal
for peace.[11]

The most significant meeting of Nhat Hanh in the United
States, however, was not with prominent political leaders but
with a fellow monk—Thomas Merton. Although they met only
one time, their Gethsemani meeting had a profound and lasting
effect upon both men. The friendship between this Vietnamese
Buddhist monk and his counterpart, the American Christian
monk, was to become one of the great interfaith friendships of
the twentieth century.

Thich Nhat Hanh and Merton had much in common. Although
they came from different religious traditions, they nonetheless were
both monks. Each drew deeply from the well of his own spiritual
tradition, and both were open to learning from the truths of other
religions. They were both committed to peacemaking and vigor-
ously opposed to the escalating war in Vietnam.

Yet the greatest bond between Nhat Hanh and Merton may
have been even more elementary than all this. At the most basic
level they recognized the humanity of the other and of every
other human being. They saw in one another great *com-pas-
sion,* a willingness to walk alongside one another, a desire to be
of practical help to one another. This commitment to a common
humanity was to be shared not only with one another but with
men and women everywhere. They believed with every fiber of
their being in the essential unity of all humanity.

Nhat Hanh called for "engaged Buddhism," and Merton simi-
larly insisted that Christians identify with the suffering of the
world.[12] This meant the avoidance of flights from reality and an
embrace of the real world. By the early 1960s, Nhat Hanh and

Merton had both read from the writings of Dietrich Bonhoeffer, the German pastor and theologian who opposed Hitler and the Nazis. His refusal to think in pure abstractions, and to act responsibly in the concrete reality of a chaotic Germany, provoked Nhat Hanh and Merton to do the same in their contemporary setting of war and violence.[13]

This was a commitment to the real that Nhat Hanh and Merton shared. No escape into a world of abstraction was permissible. In this shared commitment Nhat Hanh found Merton to be one of the few Americans who truly grasped the awful consequences of a misguided war in Vietnam with the untold suffering it caused the Vietnamese.

By the time Nhat Hanh and Merton met, Merton had already written about his opposition to the war. First and foremost, he objected to the war on humanitarian and moral grounds. He also held to the conviction that the war only strengthened communism in Asia. It did nothing for democracy. But his protest went far beyond politics. He was deeply concerned about the destruction of a people, a culture. Such destruction could not be justified on any grounds, ideological or otherwise.

A direct and blunt statement of Merton's position can be found in his introductory essay to *Faith and Violence* entitled "Toward a Theology of Resistance":

> The use of force in Vietnam is costly and settling nothing. With incredible expense and complication, and with appalling consequences to the people we claim to be helping, we are inexorably destroying the country we want to "save."[14]

Merton's theology of love, at the heart of his own spirituality and ethics, required acts of nonviolent resistance in the face of violence. The evil that led to war must be unmasked. The madness of destroying a people in order to "save" them had to be exposed. Love demanded nothing less.

Nhat Hanh's own commitment to a life of love, compassionately lived out, was very close to what Merton envisioned as a theology of resistance. The Buddhist peace movement's commitment to nonviolence was indeed something Merton also advocated. His book *Gandhi on Non-Violence* (1965) had already linked his Christian concept of compassionate love to Gandhi's philosophy of *satyagraha*. Nhat Hanh also referred to the practice of nonviolence, or the way of compassion, as love in action. In *Love in Action* he would later write:

> The essence of nonviolence is love. Out of love and the willingness to act selflessly, strategies, tactics, and techniques for a nonviolent struggle arise naturally. Nonviolence is not a dogma; it is a process. Other struggles may be fueled by greed, hatred, fear, or ignorance, but a nonviolent one cannot use such blind sources of energy, for they will destroy those involved and also the struggle itself.[15]

Merton was in full agreement. And most especially, he agreed with Nhat Hanh's conclusion: "Nonviolent action, born of the awareness of suffering and nurtured by love, is the most effective way to confront adversity."[16]

Nhat Hanh's compassionate Buddha and Merton's loving Christ had led them to the same place. Violence—in this case, the organized violence of the state called war—was contrary to the spiritual pathways they walked, whether Merton's emphasis on the Christlike life or Nhat Hanh's assumption of the Buddha-nature. In the end it was Christ's love and Buddha's compassion that drove these two monks to advocate for nonviolent approaches to conflict rather than violent confrontations.

On the most personal level, Merton's opposition to the Vietnam War was solidified in his meeting with Thich Nhat Hanh. Nhat Hanh incarnated for Merton the Vietnamese people and their suffering. They became real people to him instead of the "collateral damage" in the villages and countryside reported by the military and Pentagon officials.

Soon after their meeting Merton wrote a brief reflection about Nhat Hanh and the war entitled "Nhat Hanh Is My Brother."[17] Patrick F. O'Connell has called this eloquent statement "a declaration on human solidarity with those suffering in the war."[18] In this compassionate essay Merton brings home to the reader the reality of the Vietnam War and its suffering by speaking directly about his spiritual brother, Thich Nhat Hanh. His new brother was no abstraction, just as the war with its carnage was no abstraction. Merton could no longer keep the war at arm's length— if he ever could. He was confronted with his brother's needs. Once the human face of war is seen, it can no longer be viewed simply in terms of strategies and statistics.

Out of compassion, Merton could not turn away from Nhat Hanh and all he represented. To turn from Nhat Hanh would be for him to turn from all those in need, and from his own true self, and most especially from God. He appealed to his readers:

> He [Nhat Hanh] represents the young, the defense-
> less, the new ranks of youth who find themselves
> with every hand turned against them except those
> of the peasants and the poor, with whom they are
> working. . . . If I mean something to you, then let
> me put it this way; do for Nhat Hanh whatever you
> would do for me if I were in his position. In many
> ways I wish I were.[19]

"Do for Nhat Hanh whatever you would do for me," pleaded Merton. He was applying the Golden Rule in a personal and universal way; in the end it is God's compassionate love for all peoples that must prevail over ideologies and political expediencies of any sort.

Thomas Merton and Thich Nhat Hanh

Merton, like Nhat Hanh, extended his notion of brotherhood and sisterhood to include all humanity. In Nhat Hanh, Merton had found yet another kindred spirit, another sign of peace. He wrote of this Vietnamese monk, "He is more my brother than many who are nearer to me by race and nationality because he and I see things exactly the same way. He and I deplore the war that is ravaging his country."[20]

Merton, once again, because of an interfaith friendship extended the boundaries of love in very specific terms—to the point that compassion had no limits and love erased all boundaries. Nothing could come between them in this kind of friendship. It was based on a love that would not look away from reality. It looked directly at it. Merton knew Nhat Hanh very well:

> I have said Nhat Hanh is my brother and it is true. We are both monks and we have lived the monastic life about the same number of years. We are both poets, both existentialists.[21]

The truth is that in their shared humanity and compassion they were indeed brothers.

The Letters—a Postscript (1966)

The actual correspondence between Merton and Nhat Hanh begins after their Gethsemani meeting. In many ways, it is a postscript to a friendship already established. Neither man had much time for letter writing in the summer of 1966 following their May encounter. Merton, for his part, was busy as usual with his many writing projects, and he found his personal life complicated by his surprising, and often confusing, love for Margie, a young student nurse in Louisville.

Nhat Hanh, at the same time, discovered he could not reenter Vietnam and was exiled in France. The South Vietnamese government had declared Nhat Hanh to be a traitor to his country on the very day that he had presented his peace proposal in Washington, D.C. He was confronted with an impossible dilemma as a Buddhist peace activist. Speaking of peace made him a dangerous man to both North and South Vietnam.

Robert H. King notes that Nhat Hanh's dilemma "is eloquently set forth in his article written for the *New York Review of Books* in June 1966." Nhat Hanh writes:

> If we openly call for peace, we are identified with the communists and the government will try to suppress us. If we criticize the communists, we find ourselves aligned with those Vietnamese who have been propagandists for the Americans.[22]

Nhat Hanh was guilty of being a peacemaker. He criticized American policy for making peaceful political dissent in Vietnam almost impossible. In Nhat Hanh's words, "Now the U.S. has become too afraid of the communists to allow a peaceful confrontation with them to take place, and when you are afraid you cannot win."[23] Prophetic words indeed.

When Merton wrote Nhat Hanh on June 29, 1966, he expected his interfaith friend to be back in Saigon. But this, as we know, was not the case. Nhat Hanh had already begun his exile. A September 3, 1966, response from Nhat Hanh informed Merton that he was in Paris and not Saigon. Merton responded on September 12 telling his fellow worker for peace, "It would probably be very wise to stay out of Vietnam."[24] He knew of the great dangers Nhat Hanh faced from all sides if he tried to return.

This quick flurry of correspondence is followed by silence between the two men. But we can imagine they remained on each other's minds and in each other's prayers. Nhat Hanh concluded his September 3 letter by telling his good friend, "Do not forget to pray everyday for us."[25] In a similar fashion, Merton assured Nhat Hanh on September 12, "I certainly do pray for you and all who are working to bring some measure of peace to Vietnam."[26]

However, Merton's efforts in behalf of Nhat Hanh and his cause extended beyond prayers. He sought to use whatever influence he had in support of Nhat Hanh. This was a very personal matter for Merton. In his first letter (June 29) Merton had been enthusiastic about Nhat Hanh's nomination for the Nobel Peace Prize. He wanted Nhat Hanh to know of his personal efforts in that regard.

> You know that the FOR [Fellowship of Reconciliation] people have nominated you for the Nobel Peace Prize. I have written a letter in support of the nomination and hope you get it. It would certainly be very satisfying to us all if you did.[27]

Even though Martin Luther King, Jr., had nominated Nhat Hanh, he was not awarded the prize.

Merton understood the symbolic importance of Nhat Hanh's nomination. There was no question in his mind that his friend and brother Nhat Hanh was one of a new breed of people who were willing to offer themselves as signs of peace for a suffering world. This indeed deserved recognition and imitation.

Merton also extended his support to Nhat Hanh by writing an introduction to the English edition of Nhat Hanh's *Vietnam: Lotus in a Sea of Fire.* In solidarity with Nhat Hanh and other Buddhist peacemakers in Vietnam, Merton suggested that their enlightened approach and nonviolent engagement were the best possible hope for ending the suffering and death in Vietnam. But such efforts required the support of others.[28] And Merton tried to give that support.

The closing part of Merton's first letter to Nhat Hanh (June 29), omitted from the published version in *Hidden Ground of Love,* speaks volumes about the spiritual kinship of these two monks. It is worth noting how personal Merton was in his "benediction" at the end of his first letter. He closes with "cordial and fraternal regards" and identifies himself to his interfaith friend as "your companion on the way."[29]

Thich Nhat Hanh truly was Thomas Merton's brother, his companion on the way. And in his letter of September 3, Nhat Hanh simply addressed Father Louis Merton as "Dear Tom."[30] He too affirmed their early and steadfast friendship. From his Paris exile he told Merton he intended to lead, and did lead, the unofficial Buddhist peace delegation to the peace talks between the United States and North Vietnam beginning in 1968. He also reported to Merton his sorrow at hearing the news of D. T. Suzuki's death. But always the focus remained Vietnam and its people's suffering.

Nhat Hanh advised Merton that he would continue his efforts to keep the world informed about the plight and suffering of the Vietnamese people.[31] Although no exchange of letters exists after the pivotal year of 1966, Merton and Nhat Hanh remained aware of each other's activities in the short time Merton had left before his death in 1968. We can only imagine the further flowering and deepening of the friendship of these two men of compassion had Merton lived longer.

As for Nhat Hanh, he now lives in southwestern France, where he founded Plum Village in the early 1980s. Crucial for this retreat center are the accommodations for short-term visitors seeking spiritual relief, for refugees in transit, and for activists in need of renewal. Thousands visit each year from diverse nationalities, races, and religions to listen to Nhat Hanh's teachings, which are built upon the "engaged Buddhism" he has emphasized since the 1960s. At the center of his spiritual direction he continues to emphasize the practice of mindfulness, with its profound awareness and appreciation for life. At the heart of it all is compassion.

Of course, we cannot claim to know what Merton would have done had he lived to old age. But I can certainly imagine a wise old Merton from time to time leaving his hermitage (wherever it might be) to spend time teaching and sharing his wisdom in a place like Plum Village, perhaps even in Plum Village itself. After all, Thich Nhat Hanh and Thomas Merton were, and remain, brothers.

The exchange of letters between Merton and Thich Nhat Hanh is quite sparse. Nonetheless, the letter written on June 29, 1966, by Merton to Nhat Hanh offers a valuable glance at a deep, interfaith friendship. As Merton notes, he thinks often of his brother Thich Nhat Hanh with "much friendship."

June 29, 1966

Dear Nhat:

I suppose you are probably back in Vietnam by now. I thought of you today because I finished your excellent little book on Buddhism today. It is really a good book, and I especially liked the chapters about contact with reality and on the way to live the inner life. John Heidbrink speaks of translating it and I certainly think it ought to be translated. Meanwhile, as I said, I will try to write a review of it for some magazine or other.

You know that the FOR people have nominated you for the Nobel Peace Prize. I have written a letter in support of the nomination and hope you get it. It would certainly be very satisfying to us all if you did.

It was a great pleasure to have you here and I hope you will return some time and stay longer. If you can send me any books on Vietnamese Buddhism in French (or English) I would be very glad to read them. More of your own work ought to be translated into western languages. I think you make very clear what Buddhism really is. And I certainly feel very strongly as you do that the essential thing is to escape ignorance and the inevitable suffering that follows from it by a real contact with things as they are, instead of an illusory relationship with the world. I think your problems with conservative and formalist religiosity are very much the same as ours in the Catholic Church. It is the same everywhere. A new mentality is needed, and this implies above all a recovery of ancient and original wisdom. And a real contact with what is right before our noses.

I certainly hope that everything goes well with you, and think of you often with much friendship. Come back and see us again, and meanwhile I hope that peace will come at last to your country. Please express my warm sentiments of brotherly solidarity to all with whom you work for the better understanding of the truth and for true peace.

With cordial and fraternal regards,

Your companion on the way,

Nine

Courage

The Merton–Yungblut Letters

*These have been terrible days for every-
one [Martin Luther King, Jr.'s death],
and God alone knows what is to come.
I feel that we have already crossed a definitive line into a more apocalyptic kind
of time. . . . We will need a lot of faith
and a new vision and courage to move in
these new and more bitter realities.*
—MERTON TO JUNE YUNGBLUT,
APRIL 9, 1968

homas Merton was devastated. Like so many others, he
had placed tremendous hope in the witness and work of
Martin Luther King, Jr. Now, an assassin's bullet had
silenced God's drum major for justice. And Merton sensed that
darker days were ahead. On the very day of Dr. King's funeral he
wrote to his Quaker friend June J. Yungblut, encouraging her to
keep faith and to persevere in the times of trial that were fast
approaching—times that would require new vision, and, above
all, courage.

Merton knew that this was no time for the faint of heart. Courage would be needed to continue to follow Dr. King's prophetic lead in the march to freedom for all God's children. In fact, Merton had predicted the coming of a time of greater social upheaval long before Dr. King's death. Many of his essays in *Seeds of Destruction* (1964), for example, had anticipated a coming crisis. He had prophesied a future in which many in the white community who had supported the civil rights movement would drop away. Merton's prophecy came true. After Dr. King's assassination, black leaders demanded more control of the movement, and many whites began to back off from their commitment to the cause.

The terrible times that Merton forecast were visible during the long, hot summer following Dr. King's death. The old coalition between white liberals and black leadership had broken down. The rise of a new, younger generation of black militants, the popularity of Malcolm X's brand of black nationalism in northern urban areas, and King's own decision to broaden the social agenda to include poverty at home and the Vietnam War abroad created great unease among white liberals. Dr. King's attack on poverty and war was perceived as a threat to the capitalist commitments and national patriotism of many white Americans. Dr. King had also become more militant on issues of race. In sum, his new agenda caused many in the white community to withdraw their support from the civil rights movement.

Merton's criticism of his white liberal friends for their withdrawal of support for the movement was very frank and direct. He accused white liberals of being soft in their commitments. In "Letters to a White Liberal," published in *Seeds of Destruction,* he had critiqued the inconsistent idealism of white liberals. According to Merton:

> It is one of the characteristics of liberals that they
> prefer their future to be vaguely predictable (just as

> the conservative prefers only a future that repro-
> duces the past in all its details), when you see that
> the future is entirely out of your hands and that you
> are totally unprepared for it, you are going to fall
> back on the past, and you are going to end up in
> the arms of the conservatives.[1]

Martin Luther King's death had indeed brought on the future
Merton feared. The situation seemed entirely out of control—
and many white liberals had quietly faded from the scene. The
period of confusion and chaos that followed called for the faith,
vision, and courage that Merton had mentioned in his letter to
June Yungblut.

Consolation

Merton wanted to get a message of personal condolence to
Coretta Scott King. He hoped that June Yungblut could assist
him in this urgent matter. Merton had known June Yungblut and
her husband, John, as reliable and dedicated interfaith friends in
the struggle for peace and social justice. As longtime members
of the Society of Friends (Quakers) and the American Friends
Service Committee, the Yungbluts had been steadfast in their
commitment to Dr. King and his nonviolent struggle against racism, poverty, and war. And although Merton knew both Yungbluts,
it was June Yungblut whom he knew best. In early 1967 they
began an exchange of letters that did not end until Merton's Asian
trip in late 1968.

Born in the American South, June Yungblut came from a very
distinguished Quaker family whose roots extended back to William Penn. June was a graduate of Keuka College in upstate New
York and had earned a master's degree at Yale University and a
doctorate in philosophy from Emory. During the time she and

Merton corresponded, June and her husband served as directors of the Quaker House in Atlanta. Previously, they had worked with the Friends World Committee in South Africa. Also, at the time of her correspondence with Merton, she was very active in the civil rights movement. It was during this period that June also became friends with the King family, especially with Coretta Scott King.

Later in life June was to become a celebrated Quaker poet. Her best-known poem became the title work of a book of poems and dance photographs called *This Is the Child* (1975). It represented her effort to bring attention to the suffering of the children of Vietnam. These innocents had become the undeserving victims of a war that June so strongly opposed. To read this poem is to know June Yungblut. Her poem memorializes a Vietnamese child whose napalmed body had become etched in her consciousness. This young girl's photograph had appeared in *Life* magazine and personified the cruelty of a war fueled by a disastrous American foreign policy.

> this is the child
> who danced naked down the road in vietnam
> her cloths torn from her body
> by frenzied fingers
> the dance of death, dürer woodcut
> etched in napalm
> come forward on the stage
>   leaping, running, mouth aflame
> we are your audience
> we watch your play
> where will it all end?[2]

As this cruel war drew to its painful conclusion, June and John Yungblut continued to witness for peace. As members of the faculty at Pendle Hill, the well-known Quaker center in

Pennsylvania, they taught about the devastating effects of war. June often spoke at conferences seeking to promote social, spiritual, and physical healing in a world torn by conflict. Like other Quakers, she encouraged people to oppose war—beginning with an examination of the violence found within their own hearts. Her earlier training in dance with Martha Graham and her later work with the Barbara Mettler studios of Creative Dance rounded out a life dedicated to beauty as well as peace.

The Merton–Yungblut Letters (1967–68)

In the correspondence of Thomas Merton and June Yungblut we discover the hearts of two gifted writers and artists who shared a common concern for a world that knew little of the things which made for beauty or peace. Merton was able to meet June and John Yungblut when they visited Gethsemani in May 1967. As a result of this meeting, John Yungblut took the initiative to arrange a similar meeting between Merton and their friend Martin Luther King, Jr. According to Michael Mott, this visit by Dr. King to Gethsemani was to be a personal retreat. It would be a welcomed time for rest and reflection. Merton hoped that he and a few friends from the Catholic peace movement might provide a relaxed setting for spiritual renewal in the life of this overworked civil rights leader and Nobel Peace Laureate. Unfortunately, Dr. King's fatal trip to Memphis negated the planned visit to Gethsemani.[3]

Instead of meeting Dr. King, Merton found himself trying to get a note of condolence to Coretta Scott King. He wrote to June Yungblut on April 5, 1968. He did not have the Kings' home address and asked his interfaith friend to get his message to Mrs. King. In his letter Merton also told June Yungblut about the unusual circumstances by which he had learned of Dr. King's murder. He heard the news about Dr. King on the car radio while returning from Lexington during a rare absence from the abbey. Merton then headed to Bardstown to spend the evening with Colonel Hawk, to share the sorrow of the news with a close African American friend. "What a terrible thing," Merton wrote, "and yet I felt that he was expecting it."[4]

At the close of this letter of April 5, Merton also reflected on King's courageous life before asking for June's assistance. The gravity of the situation was already quite clear to Merton:

> This all means something more serious than we can image. But he [Dr. King], at any rate, has done all that any man can do. It will be to his glory. Could you please pass on the enclosed note to Mrs. King? I don't have their address.[5]

Merton's desire to contact Coretta Scott King was a matter of the heart. He wanted to share in Mrs. King's sorrow in a most private manner; this was not intended as a message for public record or future publication. Instead, as a monk and a priest, Merton wrote from deep within his own grieving spirit. He longed to communicate his love to the King family, and June Yungblut was to be the channel for this love.

The central paragraph of Merton's message to Coretta Scott King is quintessential Merton. Here he speaks spirit to spirit, as one broken heart to another. He laments the loss of one of God's great servants—a man who lived his life as best he could in the imitation of Christ. Merton's words to Mrs. King were personal and, at the same time, universal. He recognized that Dr. King in all his particularity was now a universal man who belonged to the ages. Merton wrote:

> Let me only say how deeply I share your personal grief as well as the shock which pervades the whole nation. He had done the greatest thing anyone can

do. In imitation of his Master he has laid down his
life for his friends and enemies. He knew the na-
tion was under judgment and he tried everything to
stay the hand of God and man. He will go down in
history as one of our greatest citizens.[6]

On April 11 June Yungblut wrote to Merton of her own personal heartbreak. She reported how she had helped at the King
home; how she had cared for the smaller King children; how she
had herself grieved as Coretta Scott King flew to Memphis to
bring home her husband's body.[7] She told Merton of her sadness
as she observed the younger King children's inability to grasp
the full reality of the tragic situation. At the same time, she told
Merton of her tremendous admiration for Coretta Scott King's
courage. She noted how deeply Mrs. King grieved in private while
courageously displaying strength and dignity in public.[8] Merton
and Yungblut, like so many others, recognized the faithful witness of Coretta King and Martin Luther King, Jr., as they nobly
carried forth the cross of Christ.

Courage

Thomas Merton, like thousands of other admirers, celebrated
the courage of Martin Luther King, Jr. As stated earlier, he had
written Mrs. King that her husband had done "all that any man
can do." He had laid down his life for friends *and* enemies. This
was the ultimate act of love. It defined love. It was love not as the
world knows it but as God knows it, and as Christ suffered for it
on the cross. This kind of love, whose author is God, casts out all
fear. "Be not afraid" (Mt 28:10; Lk 2:10). This was the gospel of
love that Martin Luther King, Jr., embraced. It engendered what
Dr. King called "the strength to love."[9] This was the kind of love
that filled the lives of Brother Martin and Sister Coretta. It also

pervaded the lives of Merton and Yungblut. Indeed, this type of love is highly contagious.

In fact, the strength to love became a central theme in the epistolary exchanges between Merton and Yungblut. Whether they were writing about Dr. King, or the war in Vietnam, or their interest in literature, or June's postdoctoral work on Merton's writings, their correspondence was filled with God's love and the encouragement that comes with it. Be not afraid. Love will endure. Have courage. This is the prevailing tone of the Merton-Yungblut letters.

How best to witness to love? This question, at times, seemed to preoccupy Merton. He realized, as a cloistered monk, that he could not engage in public protests like Martin Luther King, Jr., or his interfaith friend June Yungblut. Merton's love for the world would need to be expressed differently. Unlike June Yungblut's nonviolent public witness for love, Merton's witness had to be a much more hidden affair. Since he was living the Trappist life, his witness to love necessitated remaining in the background. Even when the desire to act publicly for love's sake became tempting at times (as it did), Merton kept to his vow of cloistered stability. This must have been particularly difficult as love's witness for peace and justice moved so many of his friends into the cities and streets of America. But Merton simply had to stay put.

In her letter of March 2, 1968, June Yungblut mentioned several public protests against the Vietnam War in which she participated. This, I suspect, must have stirred Merton's desire to act, to join in the protests. June wrote:

> Time and events have had me in an underwater tow since your note and article arrived. I think I wrote to you about the Jeanette Rankin Brigade in Washington with 5,000 of us marching and then the arrival of our 7 Vietnamese babies for relocation, the first

so far as we know to enter the country. Since then
I've participated in the Clergy and Laymen Concerned about Vietnam conference and vigil in Washington (I led the Georgia delegation), and we've just
had Thich Nhat Hanh and Jim Forest here for a
few days.[10]

By the time he received this letter, Merton had already moved
into his hermitage at Gethsemani. Public witness was out of the
question for him. He had formally entered the eremitical life on
August 20, 1965. In fact, he had been relieved of all previous
responsibilities at Gethsemani and was now a full-time hermit.
And, indeed, this was what he wanted. Quiet and solitude. Yet,
what of the world?

Aside from the occasional visit from friends, and a few unwel-
come intruders, Merton was alone in the woods as he had long
desired. Early in August 1965 he wrote: "This life is what I have
always hoped it would be and always sought. A life of peace,
silence, purpose, meaning."[11] But this is not the whole story.

Merton still desired to keep meaningful contact with others.
(The Merton-Hinson letters we examined in an earlier chapter
confirm this.) He had become a hermit, but he had no intentions
of leaving the world completely behind. Even as he moved closer
to the eremitical life, he affirmed that "the universe is my home
and I am nothing if not a part of it."[12] His goal as a hermit was to
love the world, not to abandon it.

Then, in an unexpected turn of events, at the age of fifty-one,
Merton fell in love with a young student nurse during a hospital
stay in Louisville. His personal love for Margie completed something in Merton that had been lacking. In the end, he remained
faithful to his vocation as a monk, but the world was certainly not
something to be avoided. It took on even greater significance.
Because of Margie, Merton now knew more than ever the full
meaning of love.

Henri Nouwen has observed in *Encounters with Merton* that Merton's compassion for the world seemed to increase in direct proportion to his movement toward the eremitical life at the end of his life. Nouwen quotes from Merton's preface to the Japanese edition of *The Seven Storey Mountain* to amplify this point. Written some twenty years after the original publication of his spiritual autobiography, Merton acknowledges to his readers:

> Since that time I have learned, I believe, to look back into that world with greater compassion, seeing those in it not as alien to myself, not as peculiar and deluded strangers, but as identified with myself.[13]

As a hermit, Merton was determined to live his life in loving identification with all humanity. He would exist *for* the world and not *against* the world. He would live prayerfully in solidarity with the plight of all those who suffer. In short, the world remained very much *with* Thomas Merton in his solitude.

Responding to the many public activities June Yungblut had mentioned, Merton informed her in his letter of November 19 that he too had been invited to enter the public arena. This presented another clear test for Merton's understanding of his calling to be a hermit. Should he actually enter public life for love's sake?

Merton had been asked by the American Friends Service Committee of Philadelphia to join an international peace delegation. This unofficial group was to meet with the National Liberation Front (the Vietcong) in either Cambodia or Czechoslovakia. Merton was certain that his abbot would deny him permission to participate. But he wondered whether or not to press the point. He knew this political activity would be viewed by the abbot as a worldly distraction for Gethsemani's first hermit. Yet, he could not help but wonder if his presence at the meeting might make a difference. Could he help end the war? A powerful question. The issue became moot, however, when the meeting failed to materialize.

Nonetheless, Merton felt caught once again between his commitment to solitude and his desire to act in public for love's sake. In his November 19 letter to June Yungblut he spoke of the personal dilemma that this invitation presented. In fact, it was a dilemma that was part of the paradox which was Merton's life. He noted:

> The paradox is that it is to a great extent because I am here [at the hermitage] that I am invited to go, while it is because I am here I can't go.[14]

Merton understood, somewhere deep within his spiritual bones, that to maintain credibility and remain true to himself, he could not deny his monastic and eremitical calling. He must remain cloistered as a professed hermit. Each day choices had to be made in this regard. Commitments had to be honored. Authenticity had to be maintained.

In the final analysis Merton knew that he could only speak a word of truth to the world if he remained true to his calling. Others might be called to be social activists, but this was not his charism. Others, like June Yungblut, had a God-given mandate to take their prophetic witness into the public square. However, Merton understood that he had a different divine mandate. God had called him to another kind of witness. His calling was to remain backstage, even when the urgency of the moment invited his presence on center stage. His witness was to arise from his hiddenness.

This does not mean that Merton lacked courage to act. Just the opposite. It would have been easier, given Merton's personality, to act publicly. But his actions had to come from his writing. By definition, this was a more indirect form of action. His witness was active through the written word. It is in his books, his journals, and his letters that we meet the hidden man of conviction and encouragement who June Yungblut knew from their correspondence.

Encouragement

Merton's witness was that of an encourager of faithful action. In *Contemplation in a World of Action* (1971), published after his death, we find Merton prepared to sound the call for loving action on the part of contemplatives and non-contemplatives alike. His words here are an encouragement to every person of conscience. Monk or otherwise, Merton wrote, we must make conscious choices regarding how we are to live and love. We all must act. But what form will those actions take, and are they loving?

Merton, the encourager, indicated that the only real issue for us is love. How best can we act in love? According to Merton, "To choose the world is to choose to do the work I am capable of doing, in collaboration with my brother, to make the world better, more free, more just, more livable, more humane."[15] In short, we are to become instruments of God's love, as his Franciscan friends would say. The mode of our activities may vary, but the goal is always the same—to love more completely. This is our true job description as human beings, and we cannot escape this divine mandate any more than Jonah could escape God's call to love the people of Nineveh.

This was the message that Merton and June Yungblut shared in an age of action. Keep faith! Keep on loving! Keep the witness for peace and justice alive! This was the message Merton repeated hundreds of times. Indeed, many have testified, for the record, about this great gift of encouragement so manifest in Merton.[16] And it is precisely as an encourager that Merton was experienced by June Yungblut.

In March 1968, Merton and Yungblut entered a dialogue of great importance for their letter writing. Recent events in June Yungblut's life had made her aware of changes in her spirituality; it was growing and expanding. Merton was delighted to read of this news and responded with great encouragement. He was quick to affirm the changes in his Quaker friend as she embraced a new religious consciousness.

The reason for this change was the visit of Thich Nhat Hanh to Atlanta in 1967. June had written to Merton that Nhat Hanh "was exhausted and ill" from his whirlwind speaking tour when he arrived in Atlanta. But, she added, "here at the house [Quaker House] he ate and slept well for the first time in a month."[17] Relaxed and rested, Nhat Hanh was able to be fully himself. And he made a lasting impression upon June Yungblut. In fact, his observations changed the way Yungblut viewed herself and the way she looked at the world about her.

Nhat Hanh's words on Buddhism and the war in Vietnam spoke directly to June Yungblut's heart. She was inspired by his words and his courageous witness. This all led to a reconsideration of her own spiritual journey. Yungblut told Merton that Jim Forest, their mutual friend and Catholic peace activist, was also deeply moved by Nhat Hanh's reflections. She reported to Merton that "under the sway" of Nhat Hanh she had begun to think about a new kind of religious community. With great enthusiasm she told Merton how she had discussed these matters with Jim Forest.

Now, Yungblut wanted to share these thoughts with Merton, who acted, in this case, as her spiritual adviser. She wrote to Merton on March 2, 1968, concerning all the changes she was experiencing. She reported to Merton:

> I told Jim [Forest] I had always considered myself a
> kind of Catholic Quaker. Jim answered that he had
> always considered himself a kind of Quaker Catholic

> but since he too was under the sway of Nhat Hanh,
> we would have to form a Buddhist-Quaker-
> Catholic church in Diaspora.[18]

June Yungblut's spirituality had grown in ways she may never have anticipated. Merton was intrigued (and pleased) by June's new spiritual identity and Jim Forest's notion of a "Buddhist-Quaker-Catholic church in Diaspora."

On March 6, Merton wrote back to June Yungblut and encouraged her in her new spiritual breakthrough. He liked the new interfaith formulation of Yungblut and Forest. He responded, in part, by telling June Yungblut of his own expanded spirituality. He confessed to her: "As a Catholic Buddhist of long standing and also in fact a Quaker, I naturally feel happy about the new church."[19] Merton fully endorsed the "new church" and Yungblut's own sense of her spiritual transformation. In so doing, he reaffirmed the same universal vision he had encouraged in other interfaith friends.

Merton's vision, of course, was not of a new church in any formal sense, but rather of a fellowship of interfaith friends willing to become signs of peace for the good of all. This kind of fellowship of the spirit was very much akin to the Beloved Community of Dr. King. Merton, like King, believed that God was bringing forth a new kind of spiritual frontier—a peaceable kingdom. It only remained for more and more of God's children to catch the vision and make it a more complete reality.

In Merton's mind June Yungblut was already a part of this new, emerging frontier. Although there was much evidence to the contrary, this God-inspired kingdom was clearly on its way. Peacemakers like June Yungblut had already landed on the beachheads of a warring world. Soon the world would be transformed—God willing.

Merton, as a spiritual encourager, continued to speak of a God of love and justice who would not be denied. Be not afraid.

A new day is dawning. It may be delayed, but it cannot be denied. The future belongs to God—a future that prophetic individuals like Merton, Martin Luther King, Jr., and Coretta Scott King, and Merton's interfaith friend June Yungblut anticipated in their every waking moment. More and more pioneers of this Beloved Community were stepping forward.

Strength to Love

Work for God's kingdom would, of course, requires the necessary strength to love. There is always a price to be paid by those who labor for the Beloved Community. Martin Luther King, Jr., and Coretta Scott King knew this. So did Thomas Merton and June Yungblut. It has always been so—the Hebrew prophets and Jesus also knew this quite well. Costly grace must always replace cheap grace if God's work is to be done.[20]

At the close of this chapter we return to where it began. We remember once again Martin Luther King, Jr.—one of God's great witnesses. It was his "moral imperative of love" that inspired June Yungblut and thousands of others, including Merton.[21] In a foreword to the 1982 edition of *Strength to Love,* Coretta Scott King quotes from her husband's speech to the antiwar group Clergy and Laity Concerned and reminds us of the power of Dr. King's words. These words, perhaps better than any others, express his faith in the universal nature of God's love. They also go to the core of Thomas Merton's understanding of love. In fact, Dr. King's words could have been spoken by Thomas Merton himself. King declared:

> When I speak of love I am not speaking of some
> sentimental and weak response. I am speaking of
> that force which all of the great religions have seen
> as the unifying principle of life. Love is somehow

the key that unlocks the door which leads to ultimate reality. This Hindu-Moslem-Christian-Jewish-
Buddhist belief about ultimate reality is beautifully
summed up in the first epistle of Saint John: "Let
us love one another; for love is of God and everyone that loveth is born of God and knoweth God."[22]

Love has no equal. The courage to love has no equal. Martin
Luther King, Jr., and Coretta Scott King had this love and this
courage. So did Thomas Merton and his interfaith friend June
Yungblut. Each in his or her own way. These pioneers of peace
knew of the courage to love firsthand. They all embraced love as
a "Hindu-Moslem-Christian-Jewish-Buddhist belief." This kind of
love exists without boundaries; its only limitations are the ones
that we mortals place upon it.

Ultimately, Thomas Merton and June Yungblut believed in Dr.
King's kind of love because it was of God. Nothing, not even our
own shortcomings, can keep us from this love. If we truly desire
it, God will grace us with this love and grant us the courage that
accompanies it. This is the great truth that Thomas Merton and
June Yungblut shared through their correspondence. It is so
simple, and yet so challenging. Be not afraid. Have courage.
Love.

While the letter from Merton to June Yungblut begins with news of a flu epidemic at Gethsemani and makes reference to their shared literary interests, the most significant part of this letter between interfaith friends refers to a potential visit by Martin Luther King, Jr., to the Abbey of Gethsemani, to be coordinated by June and John Yungblut.

Jan. 20, 1968

Dear June:

Beckett arrived in the midst of a flu epidemic and so it happened that last night, being holed up here in the woods and unable to sleep, I finally hoisted my ruined frame out of bed, opened up the mass wine and the Beckett underground xerox special. Great midnight illumination. The book is every bit as good as Dubliners and perhaps better. Anyhow I like it better.

The writing is superb. Dante and the Lobster is a perfect piece of work, and shattering. Much to be said about all the loneliness stuff, solitude and society and so forth throughout the book. And merciful Mother Church (Ding Dong). The whole question of mercy, suffering. I mean, is the man such a cur if he demands that after all those who talk about mercy finally mean something by it? And if he declines

COURTESY OF PENELOPE YUNGBLUT

John and June Yungblut

to be convinced by their protestations in dead language? (By which I don't mean Latin, either). I can use Belacqua in the study I am supposed to do on Camus's Stranger. Much more alive than Meursault. More about it all later. Still flung face down with the flu.

About the other letter: of course we are available any time to any one wanting to make a retreat, and if Dr King prefers to come before the march, well and good, fine with us. The only thing was that from the long term viewpoint, since the new Abbot opened our first official conversation in his new capacity by saying he wanted me to stick to my bloody mysticism and not get involved in all them outward works, it might be well to go a little slow on anything that might signify a tie in with some onslaught on the bastions of squaredom. He is essentially open, just inexperienced and still a little closed in on set positions, but I think he can learn, given time. To have Dr King, Vincent Harding and others here later in the year for a quiet, informal, deeply reflective session would probably get the Abbot to see where I really do belong, half way between in and out of the action. Not just all the way out.

No more. I go to fling this at the beadles and get supplies of orange juice and return. Wait til I learn to make one of those sandwiches Belacqua lived on: life will know no restrictions. (Except of course that cheese makes me sick).

My best to you both and to all associates,
in the Lord,

Ten

Unity

The Merton—Dona Luisa Coomaraswamy Letters

*Ananda Coomaraswamy is in many ways
to me a model: the model of one who
has thoroughly and completely united in
himself the spiritual tradition and atti-
tudes of the Orient and of the Christian
West, not excluding also something of
Islam, I believe.*

—MERTON TO DONA LUISA COOMARASWAMY,
JANUARY 13, 1961

Our closing chapter begins with a remarkable claim made
by Thomas Merton. He finds in Ananda Coomaraswamy
the model of spiritual unity that he had been seeking.
He writes Coomaraswamy's widow, Dona Luisa, that he has
discovered in Coomaraswamy's work someone who in his own
life was able to unite "all that is best and most true in the various great spiritual traditions."[1] These are the very people that
Merton celebrated at the close of his life—individuals who could
act as signs of peace for the rest of us. These were Merton's
interfaith friends. They were men and women willing to assume

the responsibility of preparation for a new kind of future, people willing to plant "new seeds of thought."

Merton, of course, viewed his own life and work as a part of this preparation. "Our task," he wrote Dona Luisa Coomaraswamy, "is one of very remote preparation, a kind of arduous and unthankful pioneering."[2] These pioneers, including Merton, have been the focus of this book. And our list of interfaith pioneers would be incomplete without Ananda and Dona Luisa Coomaraswamy.

In a very real sense the life and thought of Ananda and Dona Luisa Coomaraswamy bring together many of the themes common to Merton's own interfaith perspective. Perhaps these themes could best be organized around the motif of unity. *Unity* here does not mean uniformity or conformity. Merton would reject any such notion. The exchange of letters between Merton and Dona Luisa Coomaraswamy speak of another sort of unity—a special unity achieved only through the honest recognition of differences as well as commonalities.

Ananda K. Coomaraswamy (1877–1947)

Who was Ananda K. Coomaraswamy? Before examining the Merton–Dona Luisa Coomaraswamy letters, we need to answer this question, because it provides the historical and spiritual context for understanding their exchange. It was Merton's desire to write about Ananda Coomaraswamy that prompted his correspondence with Dona Luisa in the first place.

Ananda Kentish Coomaraswamy was born in Ceylon (present-day Sri Lanka) to a Hindu legislator and his English wife. Educated in England, he earned the degree of doctor of geology from London University before returning to his homeland in 1902. While practicing his profession as a geologist, Coomaraswamy became interested in the indigenous, pre-colonial culture of his island home. In 1908 he published *Medieval*

Sinhalese Art, a ground-breaking work in which he explored the existence of a traditional and inherently religious art in the history and culture of Ceylon.[3]

Roger Lipsey, editor of a three-volume collection of Coomaraswamy's works, notes that it was not long before this professional geologist realized his life's true vocation as an interpreter of East Indian art, culture, and religion to the Western

Ananda K. Coomaraswamy

world. He left Ceylon as a young man for the larger world of India, where he became a good friend of the poet Rabindranath Tagore. Like Tagore, he became an advocate of home rule for the Indian subcontinent. More publications, this time on Indian art and culture, followed in the ensuing years.

In 1913 Coomaraswamy began to publish in the areas of Hinduism and Buddhism. His book *Buddha and the Gospel of Buddhism* (1916) represents a pioneering publication on Buddhism geared for the general public in both the East and the West. During this decade Coomaraswamy maintained a home in England and traveled frequently between Europe and Asia. In 1918 his first American publication, *The Dance of Shiva,* appeared. Reprinted in 1957, it was to find an enthusiastic reader in Thomas Merton. Coomaraswamy's perspective on modernity in *The Dance of Shiva* was very compatible with Merton's own concerns about the quantification and compartmentalization of knowledge found among modern Western thinkers. Coomaraswamy observed:

Where the Indian mind differs most from the average mind of modern Europe is in its view of the
value of philosophy. In Europe and America the
study of philosophy is regarded as an end in itself,
and as such it seems of but little importance to the
ordinary man. In India, on the contrary, philosophy
is not regarded primarily as a mental gymnastic but
rather, and with deep religious conviction, as our
salvation (moksha) from the ignorance (avidya) which
forever hides from our eyes the vision of reality.[4]

With his move to the United States in 1917 *The Dance of Shiva*
quickly established Coomaraswamy's reputation as both a scholar
of Indian art and culture and as a popular writer on Hinduism
and Buddhism. From 1917 to 1931 Coomaraswamy served as a
curator of Indian and Muslim art at the Museum of Fine Arts in
Boston. At this time a profound transformation in Coomaraswamy's thinking began to occur. By 1932, according to Lipsey,
Coomaraswamy had turned his attention to the life of the spirit:

The art historian ceded some ground to the religious thinker and philosopher; the scientist ceded
to the man of conviction, who contrasted the secular, industrialized way of life in the modern world
with the traditional order of life in which knowledge is primarily religious and art is visible religion.[5]

Two works from this period of Coomaraswamy's life became
quite familiar to Merton: *The Transformation of Nature in Art*
(1934) and *Am I My Brother's Keeper?* (1947). These works
helped convince Merton that Ananda Coomaraswamy was the
model of spiritual unity he had been seeking. In these books
Coomaraswamy made clear his commitment to what has often

been called the perennial philosophy. He promoted a universal point of view. *All* the great religions in their own way pointed to the same Ultimate Reality—God. This included, of course, Christianity. The only problem he had with Christianity was its exclusive claim to truth. He writes, "The one outstanding, and perhaps the only, real heresy of modern Christianity in the eyes of other believers is its claim to exclusive truth." However, for Coomaraswamy, Christianity was at its roots far more inclusive than exclusive. He reminds his readers of Saint Ambrose's well-known gloss on 1 Corinthians 12:3, "All that is true, *by whomsoever it has been said,* is from the Holy Ghost."[6] Truth is truth no matter what its source. For Coomaraswamy, it can be gathered from many different cultures and religions. Drawing on the *Bhagavad Gita* in Hindu tradition, Coomaraswamy quotes Sri Krishna: "If any lover whatsoever seeks with faith to worship any form [of God] whatever, it is I who am the founder of his faith."[7] The great "I Am" appears in many forms indeed. But, for Coomaraswamy it is always the One and Same God—if it is truly God.

Turning again to Christian sources, Coomaraswamy argues for ancient Christianity's compatibility with his perennial philosophy, with his form of universalism. In "Paths That Lead to the Same Summit," a key chapter from *Am I My Brother's Keeper?,* he writes:

> We have the word of Christ himself that he came to call, not the just, but sinners (Matthew 9:13). What can we make of that, but that, as St. Justin said, "God is the Word of whom the whole human race are partakers, and those who lived according to Reason are Christians even though accounted atheists . . . Socrates and Heraclitus, and the barbarians, Abraham and many others."[8]

In sum, Coomaraswamy argues that all the great spiritual teachings ultimately speak of the same Truth. And he claims that this one Truth, God, is available to all—if we could only be awakened to this eternal truth. It is time, according to Coomaraswamy, that modern men and women remember the Truth so evident in traditional art and religion, the Truth that unites us all in love.

Coomaraswamy uses the metaphor of the mountain's summit to speak of our common spiritual goal:

> There are many paths that lead to the summit of one and the same mountain; their differences will be the more apparent the lower down we are, but they vanish at the peak; each will naturally take the one that starts from the point at which he finds himself; he who goes round about the mountain looking for another is not climbing.[9]

Since our ascent is to the same mountain summit, we ought to respect each other's climbing efforts. For Coomaraswamy, it makes no sense to tell one another how to ascend the mountain. We should certainly encourage one another, but we ought not insist that all others do it our way. In the words of this "climber" from Ceylon:

> Never let us approach another believer to ask him to become "one of us," but approach him with respect as one who is already "one of His," who is, and from whose invariable beauty all contingent being depends.[10]

We are already one of God's, to use Coomaraswamy's language. There is no need to recruit but only to climb (with God's grace).

The Merton—Dona Luisa Coomaraswamy Letters

Ananda Coomaraswamy's life and writings stimulated Merton to contact his widow in hopes that he might share her husband's philosophy about our essential unity in God with his readers. Merton, as we have seen in his first letter to Dona Luisa on January 13, 1961, paid great tribute to the memory of Ananda Coomaraswamy, someone he believed to be a true model for interreligious understanding and the advancement of world peace. Dona Luisa initially expressed reservations about focus being placed upon her late husband rather than upon his work.

Even before the January 13, 1961, letter from Merton, she had written to him about her desire to emphasize her husband's philosophy instead of his person. She had learned from a mutual friend about Merton's proposed project and wanted to ensure this sort of focus. On December 24, 1960, she had written to Merton:

> AK Coomaraswamy would object to anything "personal" as such, but not if this made possible furthering the understanding of what he wrote which (was) is not his, but everyman's, yours and mine.[11]

Merton fully agreed. After all, he felt the same way about his own writing.[12] Attention is to be given to the message not the messenger.

In his January 13 letter Merton is very sensitive to Dona Luisa's concern:

> It is not that I want to write about AKC, but rather that I want to enter contemplatively into the world

> of thought which, as you so rightly say, is for all of
> us, is not any private property of his, but which
> nevertheless had to be opened to us by him.[13]

With this kind of response, Merton had demonstrated once again
his remarkable ability to meet another person at that person's
specific point of need. Dona Luisa wanted to ensure that her
husband's legacy was properly preserved, and Merton wanted to
honor that request.

Much to his delight Merton discovered that Dona Luisa herself was an interfaith pioneer, who, like her husband, was prepared to spread "new seeds of thought." Born in 1905 to Jewish
parents in Argentina, Dona Luisa had come to the United States
at the age of sixteen. She worked as a Boston society photogra-
pher and married Ananda Coomaraswamy in 1930. At her
husband's suggestion Dona Luisa studied Sanskrit and popular
folklore in India for more than two years. After this she worked
closely with her husband as his academic and literary secretary.
After his death she began gathering and editing his papers for a
definitive edition of his writings. It was at this point that the Merton
correspondence began. Dona Luisa died in 1970.[14]

Merton must have known a few of the essentials of Dona Luisa's
life before he first wrote her. He seemed to understand that she
would be quite interested in his contemplative approach to her
husband's writings. Merton's language is almost lyrical, and certainly heart-felt, as he described to Dona Luisa his proposed approach to Ananda Coomaraswamy's work:

> The study of AKC will be reserved for a very pleas-
> ant hermitage among the pine trees, looking over
> the valley, a place which I think would have ap-
> pealed to him and where I now spend much time,
> when I can.[15]

In this brief statement Merton presented himself as a monk first and a writer second. He knew that Dona Luisa would appreciate a contemplative approach to the understanding of Ananda Coomaraswamy's message. However, Merton was in no hurry. As a good Trappist, he had no need to press ahead for the sake of expediency. He wrote to Dona Luisa:

> Please feel perfectly free to refuse me anything, to take your time in answering any letters, and do not be disturbed if my requests may accidentally and unintentionally seem importunate. I do not want to badger you or impose on your kindness, and really what is important is not that I be able to "get information" or "borrow books" but rather that I may have the joy and the privilege of a living contact with you and thus with AKC and his world of thought.[16]

Merton genuinely sought "the privilege of a living contact" with Dona Luisa and her husband's work. As in his other interfaith contacts, connection on the personal level was far more important than any formal dialogue on the level of philosophical or theological doctrines. What Merton truly desired was a direct spiritual engagement with Ananda Coomaraswamy. He wrote Dona Luisa, "I cannot help but feel that his 'world of thought' is also mine, and that in any other realm today I am purely and simply an exile." It was indeed a personal matter for Merton. He wanted to enter the spiritual territory of Ananda Coomaraswamy. Merton tells Dona Luisa, "Forgive me then, all I really ask is an opportunity to feel myself a citizen of my true country."[17]

The "true country" that Merton shared with Ananda and Dona Luisa Coomaraswamy was a homeland free of religious manipulation of people into places they did not want to go. In Ananda

Coomaraswamy's efforts to interpret Indian culture to the West, he had emphasized the need for spiritual freedom.

> The heart and essence of the Indian experience is to be found in a constant intuition of the unity of all life, and the instructive and ineradicable conviction that the recognition of this unity is the highest good and the uttermost freedom.[18]

This "uttermost freedom" was not to be abridged by those who would deny others the very freedom they desired for themselves.

According to Ananda Coomaraswamy: "All that India can offer to the world proceeds from her philosophy [spiritual freedom]." It comes as India's gift to the world but is not totally unknown outside India. He writes:

> This philosophy is not, indeed, unknown to others—it is equally the gospel of Jesus and of Blake, Lao Tzu and Rumi—but nowhere else has it been made the essential basis of sociology and education [and the spiritual traditions of Hinduism and Buddhism].[19]

The West, according to Coomaraswamy, can learn much from India's spiritual inclusiveness.

Influenced by her husband's universal perspective, Dona Luisa wrote the following to Merton in her letter of January 23, 1961:

> I personally do not hold to converting, because of this, what is con-genial to us may not be truly so to another, on our level of reference, I trust. I do hold with the possibility of any individual after some 18–20 years study, one Avitar may come to be more apparent (to one present-being) than another, but

> after 18–20 years of study . . . we should have come
> to be God's very own in whatever channel it has
> pleased Him to cast us in.[20]

Dona Luisa, like her husband, had confidence that God leads each of us in the proper way. If we remain spiritually attentive, the path will become clear. Merton expressed his agreement with Dona Luisa in his letter of February 12, 1961. He notes, "Like you, I hate proselytizing." The whole matter was distasteful for Merton: "This awful business of making others just like oneself so that one is thereby 'justified' and under no obligation to change himself. What a terrible thing this can be. The source of how many sicknesses in the world."[21]

Proselytizing, of course, has not ceased. Often times Christianity is guilty of this practice. But fundamentalists of all sorts, in so many different religions, are the prime offenders—seeking to make others over into themselves. In his words to Dona Luisa, Merton offered a far different message. As a Christian monk he writes:

> The true Christian apostolate is nothing of this sort,
> a fact which Christians themselves have largely for-
> gotten. I think it was from Ananda that I first heard
> the quote of Tauler (or maybe Eckhart) who said in
> a sermon that even if the church were empty he
> would preach the sermon to the four walls because
> he had to. That is the true apostolic spirit, based
> not on the desire to make others conform, but in
> the desire to proclaim and announce the good tid-
> ings of God's infinite love.[22]

The proclaimer is not a "converter" for Merton. One who proclaims is rather a "herald, a voice *(kerux),* and the Spirit of the Lord is left free to act as He pleases." However, for Merton, much of modern religion has degenerated into "convert-makers" who use every technique of human manipulation available, and in the process, program out the Holy Spirit altogether. In a devastating indictment Merton declares to Dona Luisa, "Little do men realize that in such a situation the Holy Spirit is silent and inactive, or perhaps active *against* the insolence of man."[23]

Ananda Coomaraswamy and Dona Luisa Coomaraswamy had a genuine desire to spread the message of God's love in a universal way—devoid of manipulation and control. For Merton, this was a central thread woven throughout his contacts with all his interfaith friends. People must be free to be who they truly are—children of the one God. Merton tells Dona Luisa that Ananda Coomaraswamy was

> a voice bearing witness to the truth, and he wanted nothing but for others to receive that truth in their own way, in agreement with their own mental and spiritual context. As if there were any other way of accepting it. But no, this awful mistake of the west, which is certainly not a "Christian" mistake at all, but the fruit of western aggressivity, was the idea that one had to "convert" the east and make it change in every way into a replica of the west. This is one of the great spiritual crimes of man.[24]

Merton, like Ananda Coomaraswamy, insisted that God's love could not be a Western possession. In its own spiritual and cultural idiom, the East also knew of God's Reality. And indeed, the East has much to teach the West about the Universal. This is not because the East is wiser than the West. Rather, it is because the East is older and therefore more experienced in spiritual matters. "If we regard the world as a family of nations," observed Ananda Coomaraswamy, "then we shall best understand the position of India which has passed through many experiences and solved many problems which younger races have hardly yet recognized."[25]

There Comes a Time

To sharpen the Western world's spiritual awareness, Dona Luisa wondered if something like a Sufi order could be established in Christianity. Writing Merton on January 23, 1961, she noted that "there comes a time" in which "only the top-values survive" in a culture. Perhaps this time had come for the West.[26] Just as the Sufis had enlivened a stagnant Islam, Dona Luisa wondered whether a similar thing could not happen in Christianity. Merton responded favorably, but with a word of caution. He wrote to Dona Luisa on February 12, 1961:

> You are right about the Sufis and about the need for Christian equivalents of the Sufis. This kind of need is not something that man thinks up and then takes care of. It is a question of God's honor and glory and of His will. Men do not choose to be Sufis; least of all Christian Sufis so to speak: they are chosen and plunged into the crucible like iron into the fire.[27]

Merton himself knew what it was like to be "chosen and plunged into the crucible like iron into the fire." Indeed, the role of the prophet in response to God's calling was often complex and confusing. Merton understood how pioneers of faith, like himself and his interfaith friends, live under "the sign of contradiction."[28] Like Jonah, they are frequently compelled to speak and act in ways that are not totally clear to them—and certainly not to others. A Christian Sufi order? Perhaps, but it must come from God; it cannot be any kind of human invention.

Yet, one thing was clear. In Dona Luisa and Ananda Coomaraswamy, Merton had discovered pioneers willing to work for global peace rather than global destruction—interfaith pioneers willing to be signs of peace. Of himself, Merton wrote, "Would that I might so live gently, non-violently, firmly, in all humility and meekness, but not betraying the truth."[29] God was, as always, the source of this truth. Dona Luisa wrote to Merton:

> There are no exclusions—where man is God IS—
> and this applies to the so-called 'barbarians' in the
> remotest parts of the world. . . . There is no mo-
> nopoly on MONOtheism, never was—can you imag-
> ine God objecting, in any way whatever, to what
> Names He is called! Or what forms one worships
> Him in. Let us not attribute to Him our shortcom-
> ings.[30]

God may have a thousand different names, but God remains One. God cannot be limited by the official doctrines or dogma of any religious group. For Dona Luisa, "The way is multiple, 'He is multiple, as He is in us, at the same time, He is Unity so He is in Himself. Many are called, few are ready, and even of these, fewer are chosen.'"[31] The few, however, can become the many. But for this to happen, the prophetic few, the new interfaith pioneers, must continue to profess and embody the God of a thousand different names. Dona Luisa was well aware that she and her husband had taken on the "arduous and unthankful pioneering" effort identified by Merton. She, like her husband, was fully committed to spiritual unity within the world's religions—even if few were prepared to listen. The new day was coming.

Without question, Merton affirmed Dona Luisa's philosophy of spiritual unity. From the start of their correspondence he had identified himself as a Christian monk. He had told Dona Luisa, "I am speaking not as a writer [the way in which Dona Luisa would have known of Merton] but rather a monk."[32] From his monastic perspective Merton saw himself as a fellow pilgrim with Dona Luisa who, like her, sought God in the shared experiences of the world's religions. Here they agreed.

But was Merton's Christian viewpoint nonetheless delimiting? Not in the broadest sense. It was precisely because he was a Christian monk, and not in spite of it, that he worked for the spiritual unity that Dona Luisa espoused. Merton wrote to her: "I am deliberately concentrating . . . orienting my life or letting it be oriented in a direction in which I write no more books, and write nothing except what writes itself unsystematically and spontaneously.[33] Merton had reached the point in his life at which he was prepared to forego all other activities for the sake of a global unity in God. It was along these lines that Merton wrote "unsystematically and spontaneously" to Dona Luisa on September 24, 1961, about his vocation to unity. He tells her:

> You must understand by now that I do not entertain formally conventional notions of the church. I certainly believe with all my heart in the Church, none more so. But I absolutely refuse to take the rigid, stereotyped, bourgeois notions that are acceptable to most Catholics and which manage in the long run to veil the true mystery of Christ and make it unattainable to some people.[34]

Merton wrote these words in response to a specific statement made by Dona Luisa in an earlier letter. She had written, "I am and I am not a Roman Catholic. . . . I may say I am catholic, but no more nor less Jewish, Muslim, Hindu, Buddhist—and Christian."[35] In his response Merton indicated that he was more in Dona Luisa's theological camp than in that of most Catholics. But he was also clear that he remained a faithful member of the church.

In Merton's response, we find the brilliant and maddening genius of his spirituality; he is and he isn't. He affirms "the true mystery of Christ," and yet he remains open to truth as it comes to him from other religions. Dona Luisa could respect and understand this. After all, she had claimed "I am and I am not a Roman Catholic." She made this claim based on her husband's universal, religious philosophy. Therefore, she could also assert with equanimity that she was "no more nor less Jewish, Muslim, Hindu, Buddhist—and Christian."

Merton, however, would have expressed his vocation to interfaith unity in a manner slightly different from Dona Luisa. His approach was dialectical, while Dona Luisa's was more syncretistic. Rather than dissolve the differences between his faith and others—as Dona Luisa tended to do—Merton chose to live within a spiritual and philosophical creative tension. The path God had granted him (life in Christ) could not be compromised. Yet at the same time the robust trajectories of other spiritual traditions also contained truth that Merton could not deny. His solution: live in the tension.

Merton agreed with Dona Luisa that God is greater than the limitations imposed by any religious system. The divine One knows of no human boundaries, especially those drawn by organized religion. And he also agreed with Dona Luisa that God moves us, almost imperceptibly, toward greater unity. However, the wellspring of Merton's insights into God remained his Christian monastic experience. In other words, universal truth was opened to Merton because of the particularity of his own faith. His rootedness in his own faith (to use another metaphor) enabled him the freedom necessary to explore what other forms of religious experience, and religions, had to teach him.

There is indeed so much to learn. As a species we have not been at this very long. Unity and genuine peace may be far beyond our present moment. But for Merton and Dona Luisa, we are on the move. According to Merton, our knowledge of God is no longer merely as though it were knowledge of an "object"! (Who could bear such a thing: and yet religious people do it: just as if the world contained here a chair, there a house, there a hill, and then again God. As if the identity of all were not hidden in Him Who has no name.)[36]

Merton concluded that God is not an object among other objects—and never has been—for those who live in the depths of their own religious traditions. Spiritual pioneers know the God who has no name. Yet, this God of no name is the God of all names. For Merton, this is none other than the God who is in Christ, but this God is none other than the God who, for Merton and his interfaith friends, is literally everywhere and nowhere.

Dona Luisa had written Merton that "there comes a time." That time is *now*. It has always been *now* for the God who loves us. Of this, those united with Merton in his spiritual quest were quite confident. Notwithstanding the fragmentation and resistance of our times, "the time has come." Why? Because, as Merton and his interfaith friends understood so well, the God of no name and of many names is eternally present. Peace will come. The One whose name is above all names—the hidden Ground of Love—ensures it. It is time, as it has always been, for those who are signs of peace to shine forth. As always, the God of Light and Love, known to Thomas Merton and Dona Luisa Coomaraswamy, will illumine the way.

*In this lengthy letter of February 12, 1961, some-
thing of the breadth and intellectual depth of
Merton's correspondence with Dona Luisa Coomaraswamy is evident. Merton's initial interest in
corresponding with Dona Luisa concerned his fascination with the work of her deceased husband,
Ananda K. Coomaraswamy, a world-renowned
scholar of Hindu religion and culture. However,
Merton's friendship with Dona Luisa took on a vi-
brant life of its own.*

Feb. 12, 1961

Dear Dona Luisa:

Many thanks for your two very rich and stimulating letters,
and the additional notes. So many wonderful openings for new
thought, study and meditation. I have meanwhile returned to
you the things you lent me first: the memorial volume and the
two or three magazines. I don't think I mentioned before that I
particularly enjoyed the Dana Lila, with Gill's illustrations, and
AKC's quote from the two carols was very inspiring to me, especially the Cornish one, "Tomorrow will be my dancing day." I
have been able to track down the one about Besse: in one version it is purely secular with no sacred reference. In a footnote
there is the piece given by AKC and a statement that it alludes to
Queen Elizabeth!! I don't see how she could be "mankinde." See
Duncan. *Lyrics from the Old Song Books* London 1927, p.
12. He says in a note (p. 13) that the bit quoted by AKC with the
obviously religious content is "a moralization on Queen Elizabeth's
accession." On the other hand I think it is the main text he gives,
with its last stanza referring to England married to Sweet Bessy,
that is obviously the reference to Elizabeth. W. Chappell in *Old
English Popular Music,* London 1893 (vol I, p. 122), makes it

clear that the non-religious text refers to Elizabeth and the religious text, quoted by AKC, is older and closer to the common source of the two which has been lost.

We have here a record of some Indian religious music, in the Folkways series, and I enjoy it very much, especially some of the popular legends, like the one about the Black parrot. But the chanting of the Vedas, of which a sample is given, was the thing that really first opened up the Upanishads to me. The *way* in which the words are chanted shows the spiritual character of Hindu singing and reflects the spiritual understanding of breath that is exposed in the Upanishads. I am now finishing the Brihad Aranyaka Upanishad and it is tremendous.

Yes, I have read Marco Pallis. We do not have it here, I borrowed it from Victor Hammer's wife (he met AKC once and has some offprints of his). I copied out some of the best bits about Tibetan art and craftsmanship (I make no distinction).

A friend of mine, Louis Massignon, one of the great scholars of Moslem mysticism, is passionately devoted to Abraham and his mystical life is all under the sign of Abraham and of the sacrifice of Isaac. Massignon is one of the few Christians I know who has really deep and warm contacts with Moslems. Through him I have met one very ardent soul in Pakistan. You are right about the Sufis and about the need for Christian equivalents of the Sufis. This kind of need is not something that man thinks up and then takes care of. It is a question of God's honor and glory and of His will. Men do not choose to be Sufis, least of all Christian Sufis so to speak: they are chosen and plunged into the crucible like iron into the fire. I do not know if I have been so chosen but I am familiar enough with the crucible, and I live under the sign of contradiction. Would that I might so live gently, non-violently, firmly, in all humility and meekness, but not betraying the truth.

But there is certainly a great need of an interior revival of truth, religious truth. There are everywhere movements which more and more seem to be simply evasions. Collective evasions,

with an enormous amount of publicity and false front, with great
numbers of speeches and conferences and publications and no
one knows what else. And little or no interior fruit, simply a
multiplication of addicts and proselytes. Like you, I hate proselytizing. This awful business of making others just like oneself so
that one is thereby "justified" and under no obligation to change
himself. What a terrible thing this can be. The source of how
many sicknesses in the world.

The true Christian apostolate is nothing of this sort, a fact
which Christians themselves have largely forgotten. I think it was
from Ananda that I first heard the quote of Tauler (or maybe
Eckhart) who said in a sermon that even if the Church were
empty he would preach the sermon to the four walls because he
had to. That is the true apostolic spirit, based not on the desire
to make others conform, but in the desire to proclaim and an-
nounce the good tidings of God's love. In this context the preacher
is not a "converter" but merely a herald, a voice *(kerux),* and the
Spirit of the Lord is left free to act as He pleases. But this has
degenerated into a doctrine and fashion of "convert-makers" in
which man exerts pressure and techniques (the awful business of
"modern techniques of propaganda") upon his fellow man in
order to make him, force him, bring him under a kind of charm
that compels him to abandon his own integrity and his own freedom and yield to another man or another institution. Little do
men realize that in such a situation the Holy Spirit is silent and
inactive, or perhaps active *against* the insolence of man. Hence
the multitude of honest and sincere men who "cannot accept" a
message that is preached without respect for the Spirit of God or
for the spirit of man.

It must have been something of this mentality which got into
the thought of good Albert Gleizes (I know of his work, he is a
good artist is he not?) when he said what he said to AKC. I
cannot conceive of that kind of contradiction because I know
that AKC was never trying to pressure anybody: he just was a

COURTESY OF RAMA COOMERASWAMY

Dona Luisa Coomeraswamy

voice bearing witness to the truth, and he wanted nothing but for others to receive that truth in their own way, in agreement with their own mental and spiritual context. As if there were any other way of accepting it. But no, this awful mistake of the west, which is certainly not a "Christian" mistake at all, but the fruit of western aggressivity was the idea that one had to "convert" the east and make it change in every way into a replica of the west. This is one of the great spiritual crimes of man in its own unconscious way and we are only beginning to reap the fruit of it in China, the Congo, etc. Have you read a wonderful book called the *Dark Eye in Africa* by Laurens Van der Post? He is another remarkable person, and on primitive man he also wrote a splendid book about the bushmen of South Africa, the *Lost World of the Kalahari*. Several other interesting books about these bushmen are appearing here and there. Most important insights into the reality of primitive man. What you quote AKC as saying about the underlying resentment and contempt in the attitude of men like Frazer and Levy Bruehl is terribly true.

Thank you for your quotes on Hebrew forms of prayer. I wish I knew Hebrew. My languages are all western. Some day I will have to start on an Oriental one but I dread it, our time for concentrated study is very short. Yet perhaps I may do it.

Did you ever get the little thing on Mencius and the offprint on "creativity"—a fashionable fetish-word these days. I hope you got the Mencius anyways, as I think you would like the way it is printed and the content of the text.

The books you said you would send, including the *Dance of Shiva,* will be most welcome when they arrive. I am profoundly grateful and look forward to them. It is good of you to put yourself out for me. I finished all the things in the memorial volume. Is Benjamin Rowland still around Cambridge? I might write to him also. What would you say AKC would have thought of abstract expressionism in art? It has much to be said in its favor, but as a fashion it is a bit obnoxious. What did he think and say about people like Picasso, who is undoubtedly a great genius . . . but perhaps that is the trouble.

Eckhart I know. We have here a popular edition of him, and I have something in French of his. I like him, and Tauler and Ruysbroeck. Do you know St John of the Cross? He is less metaphysical than the others.

I am sending you an article of mine on Chinese Thought, which Graham Carey has read. He may already have spoken to you of it, as he wrote to me about it. And a book of mine on the Psalms which goes somewhat into the different senses of Scripture you spoke of before. Yes, I agree that much ought to be done on symbolism and typology and I hope to get at it some time.

Now I must close, with always the very best wishes and cordial understanding;

Yours in the charity of Christ,

Postscript

A Small Message of Hope

And so I stand among you as one who offers a small message of hope, that first, there are always people who dare to seek on the margin of society, who are not dependent on social routine, and prefer a kind of free-floating existence under a state of risk. And among those people, if they are faithful to their own calling, to their own vocation, and to their own message from God, communication on the deepest level is possible.

—MERTON, INFORMAL TALK, CALCUTTA,
OCTOBER 1968

Like Merton, we have attempted in this volume to offer "a small message of hope." There are always the practical dreamers, in this case men and women of various faiths who stand ready to be spiritual pioneers, thinking and acting as signs of peace. In October 1968, not long before his death, Merton delivered an informal talk in Calcutta sponsored by the Temple of Understanding (an interfaith organization) in which he once again called forth those willing to communicate God's message "on the deepest level."

What is this message of God? We have heard it again and again in the correspondence of Merton and his interfaith friends. This message never seems to change or waver. It is a message that our pioneers of faith could not walk away from. It can be found in their writings and in the lives they lived. The message is not all that complicated, once seen and experienced. It is so simple, so profoundly true. And it cannot be ignored. It is the message of God's love.

Merton and his interfaith friends speak of nothing else but this message. The message is shared from one person to another. It is personal, and it defies institutionalization. Some might be tempted to make it into a slogan. It might even end up as an aphorism printed on a refrigerator magnet. But ultimately it cannot be abased or trivialized, for it is from God. Although it always rings true, its communication must be carefully cultivated. In fact, this message of love often does not come to us through "normal" channels.

Those who know it best and experience its truth communicate it in a different way—a way our interfaith friends have discovered (or rediscovered). Merton constantly reminded us of this way. It is not a new way at all, but it is a way that has largely been forgotten. It is, in fact, the way of deepest communication. Merton, as only Merton can, identifies this way in a most provocative manner:

> The deepest level of communication is not communication, but communion. It is wordless. It is beyond words, and it is beyond speech, and it is beyond concept. Not that we discover a new unity. We discover an older unity. My dear brothers, we are already one. But we imagine that we are not. And what we have to recover is our original unity. What we have to be is what we are.[1]

This is God's most essential message to us. We are already one. We are united in love. Merton and his interfaith friends knew this to be true in the very marrow of their spiritual bones. Bigotry and injustice have no place in this new (but original) way. War and violence are incompatible with God's truth. How could any of this fit God's reality (God's kingdom)? To harm another is to harm ourselves. We visit only death upon ourselves by our divisiveness. We are already one. This is the truth of God for our times—for any time.

And so God's litany of our original unity is sung (and also danced) by God's witnesses. What Merton and his interfaith friends experienced, in the end, is not new at all. We are already one. Period. "But," as Merton observed, "we imagine we are not." That is the tragedy of our day.

Yet, the world is gradually awakening. We are beginning to look differently at ourselves and others. With God's help there is the real possibility that we, at least some of us, are becoming signs of peace for our broken and violent world, a world so desperately in need of love. This is the "small message of hope" that Merton and his interfaith friends had begun to realize a half-century ago. The course is set before us. God's message is always before us and in our hands. According to Merton, "What we have to be is what we are." Signs of God's peace.

Notes

Foreword

1. Thomas Merton, *The Seven Storey Mountain* (New York: Harcourt Brace and Company, 1948), 187.

2. Thomas Merton, *Seeds of Contemplation* (New York: New Directions, 1949), 87.

3. Thomas Merton, *"Honorable Reader": Reflections on My Work*, ed. Robert E. Daggy (New York: Crossroad, 1989), 9.

4. William H. Shannon, *Silent Lamp: The Thomas Merton Story* (New York: Crossroad, 1992), 183.

5. Thomas Merton, *Conjectures of a Guilty Bystander* (Garden City, NY: Doubleday and Company, 1966), 12.

6. Ibid., 129.

7. Ibid.

8. Chakravarty to Merton, March 29, 1967, archives of the Thomas Merton Center, Bellarmine University, Louisville, Kentucky (hereafter TMC).

9. Wu to Merton, November 28, 1961 (TMC).

10. Dalai Lama, "A Tribute to Thomas Merton," in *The Gethsemani Encounter: A Dialogue on the Spiritual Life by Buddhist and Christian Monastics*, ed. Donald W. Mitchell and James Wiseman, OSB (New York: Continuum, 1999), 260–61.

Preface

1. William H. Shannon, ed., *The Hidden Ground of Love: The Letters of Thomas Merton on Religious Experience and Social Concerns* (New York: Farrar, Straus and Giroux, 1985), 126–27.

2. Ibid., 126.

3. Brother Patrick Hart, ed., *Thomas Merton, Monk: A Monastic Tribute* (Kalamazoo, MI: Cistercian Publications, 1983), 209.

4. Ibid., 212.

5. Christine M. Bochen, *Thomas Merton: Essential Writings* (Maryknoll, NY: Orbis Books, 2002), 48.

6. Shannon, *The Hidden Ground of Love,* 126.

1 Merton's Ministry of Letters

1. Paul M. Pearson suggested these figures to me in a letter dated January 21, 2005. According to Dr. Pearson, ten thousand letters is a conservative estimate based on the letters in the center's archives. It does not include letters in other collections, letters in private hands, and ones that were lost or destroyed.

2. William H. Shannon, Christine M. Bochen, and Patrick F. O'Connell, eds., *The Thomas Merton Encyclopedia* (Maryknoll, NY: Orbis Books, 2002), 255.

3. This event took place at Linfield College in September 1999. The woman and man remain anonymous.

4. William H. Shannon, "Preface," in *The Hidden Ground of Love: The Letters of Thomas Merton on Religious Experience and Social Concerns,* ed. William H. Shannon (New York: Farrar, Straus and Giroux, 1985), vi.

5. Shannon, Bochen, and O'Connell, *The Thomas Merton Encyclopedia,* 255.

6. Shannon, "Preface," vi.

7. Shannon, Bochen, and O'Connell, *The Thomas Merton Encyclopedia,* 255.

8. Robert E. Daggy, ed., "Introduction," in *Encounter: Thomas Merton and D.T. Suzuki* (Louisville, KY: Larkspur Press, 1988), xiii. Daggy provides an excellent review of the status of publications regarding Merton correspondence in the first two decades after Merton's death.

9. Ibid.

10. Ibid.

11. *Cold War Letters,* edited by William H. Shannon and Christine M. Bochen, is being published at long last by Orbis Books.

12. Daggy, "Introduction," xv–xvi.

13. Shannon, Bocher, and O'Connell, *The Thomas Merton Encyclopedia,* 255.

2 Blessings: The Merton-Aziz Letters

1. Sidney H. Griffith, "One Spiritual Man to Another: The Merton-Abdul Aziz Correspondence," in *Merton and Sufism: The Untold Story,* ed. Rob Baker and Gray Henry (Louisville, KY: Fons Vitae, 1999), 101–2.

2. A week of research in the archives of Boston University's library (on Howard Thurman's works) in April 1997 was followed by a week at the Thomas Merton Center at Bellarmine University where I began to see a connection between the notion of blessings found in the Thurman story and in the Merton-Aziz correspondence. This resulted in

my "The Merton-Aziz Letters: An Interfaith Journey toward Unity," *The Merton Seasonal* 28, no. 3 (fall 2003).

3. William H. Shannon, ed., *The Hidden Ground of Love: The Letters of Thomas Merton on Religious Experience and Social Concerns* (New York: Farrar, Straus and Giroux, 1985), 43.

4. Abdul Aziz to Merton, November 1, 1960. Abdul Aziz's letters are for the most part unpublished (except for partial quotations in *Merton and Sufism: The Untold Story*); they are kept in the archives of the Thomas Merton Center, Bellarmine University, Louisville, Kentucky (hereafter TMC).

5. Shannon, *The Hidden Ground of Love,* 44.

6. Baker and Henry, *Merton and Sufism,* 103.

7. Ibid., 103–4.

8. Christine M. Bochen, *Thomas Merton: Essential Writings* (Maryknoll, NY: Orbis Books, 2002), 48.

9. Shannon, *The Hidden Ground of Love,* 45.

10. Abdul Aziz to Merton, December 20, 1960 (TMC).

11. Shannon, *The Hidden Ground of Love,* 115.

12. Ibid., 56.

13. Ibid.

14. Baker and Henry, *Merton and Sufism,* 109.

15. Ibid., 110.

16. Ibid., 112.

17. Ibid., 112–13.

18. Abdul Aziz to Merton, December 26, 1966 (TMC).

19. Shannon, *The Hidden Ground of Love,* 46.

20. Ibid.

21. Ibid., 61.

22. Ibid.

23. Ibid., 63–64.

3 Love: The Merton-Chakravarty Letters

1. Amiya Chakravarty to Merton, March 29, 1967, archives of the Thomas Merton Center, Bellarmine University, Louisville, Kentucky (hereafter TMC).

2. Amiya Chakravarty to Merton, March 29, 1967 (TMC).

3. William H. Shannon, ed., *The Hidden Ground of Love: The Letters of Thomas Merton on Religious Experience and Social Concerns* (New York: Farrar, Straus and Giroux, 1985), 115.

4. Amiya Chakravarty to Merton, September 28, 1966 (TMC).

5. William H. Shannon, Christine M. Bochen, and Patrick F. O'Connell, eds., *The Thomas Merton Encyclopedia* (Maryknoll, NY: Orbis Books, 2002), 379.

6. Amiya Chakravarty to Merton, September 28, 1966 (TMC).

7. Amiya Chakravarty to Merton, November 30, 1966 (TMC).

8. Ibid.

9. Ibid.

10. Ibid.

11. Ibid.

12. Ibid.

13. Ibid.

14. Thomas Merton, *Zen and the Birds of Appetite* (New York: New Directions, 1968), 81.

15. Amiya Chakravarty to Merton, January 12, 1967 (TMC).

16. Shannon, *The Hidden Ground of Love,* 112.

17. Thomas Merton, *Gandhi on Non-Violence* (New York: New Directions, 1965), 51.

18. Ibid.

19. Amiya Chakravarty to Merton, January 16, 1967 (TMC). The "Merton Evening" did not happen until March 1967.

20. Ibid.

21. Ibid.

22. Ibid.

23. Shannon, *The Hidden Ground of Love,* 113.

24. Ibid., 113–14.

25. Ibid., 114.

26. Amiya Chakravarty to Merton, March 29, 1967 (TMC).

27. Shannon, *The Hidden Ground of Love,* 115.

28. Ibid.

29. Amiya Chakravarty to Merton, May 4, 1968 (TMC).

30. Shannon, *The Hidden Ground of Love,* 120.

31. Amiya Chakravarty to Merton, May 4, 1968 (TMC).

32. Thomas Merton, *The Asian Journal of Thomas Merton* (New York: New Directions, 1973), 32.

33. Amiya Chakravarty, "Preface," in Merton, *The Asian Journal of Thomas Merton,* vii.

34. Amiya Chakravarty to Merton, September 1967 (TMC).

35. Chakravarty, "Preface," vii.

36. Shannon, Bochen, and O'Connell, *The Thomas Merton Encyclopedia,* 51.

37. Thomas Merton, *Confessions of a Guilty Bystander* (Garden City, NY: Doubleday, 1966), 157.

4 Wisdom: The Merton-Wu Letters

1. John Wu to Merton, March 20, 1961, archives of the Thomas Merton Center, Bellarmine University, Louisville, Kentucky (hereafter TMC).

2. John C. H. Wu, *Beyond East and West* (New York: Sheed and Ward; Taipei: Mei Ya Publications, 1995 [1969]), 317.

3. Ibid., 149.

4. Ibid.

5. Ibid.

6. Ibid., 350.

7. John Wu visited Merton at Gethsemani during the latter part of June in 1962.

8. Wu, *Beyond East and West,* 14.

9. Ibid., 37.

10. Ibid., 243.

11. Ibid., 207–8.

12. Ibid., 244.

13. Ibid., 150.

14. Ibid., 178.

15. Ibid., 202–3.

16. Ibid., 192.

17. Ibid.

18. Ibid., 198.

19. Thomas Merton, *The Asian Journal of Thomas Merton* (New York: New Directions, 1973), 233.

20. Wu, *Beyond East and West,* 350.

21. William H. Shannon, Christine M. Bochen, Patrick F. O'Connell, eds., *The Thomas Merton Encyclopedia* (Maryknoll, NY: Orbis Books, 2002), 220.

22. William H. Shannon, ed., *The Hidden Ground of Love: The Letters of Thomas Merton on Religious Experience and Social Concerns* (New York: Farrar, Straus and Giroux, 1985), 612.

23. Ibid.

24. John Wu to Merton, March 20, 1961 (TMC).

25. Shannon, *The Hidden Ground of Love,* 612.

26. Thomas Merton, *The Way of Chuang Tzu* (New York: New Directions, 1965), 9.

27. Ibid., 20.

28. Shannon, *The Hidden Ground of Love,* 631.

29. John Wu to Merton, July 17, 1962 (TMC).

30. Shannon, *The Hidden Ground of Love,* 263.

31. Ibid., 631.

32. Ibid., 632.

33. Ibid., 633.

5 Holiness: The Merton-Heschel Letters

1. Beatrice Bruteau, ed., *Merton and Judaism: Holiness in Words* (Louisville, KY: Fons Vitae, 2003), 217–18.

2. William H. Shannon, ed., *The Hidden Ground of Love* (New York: Farrar, Straus and Giroux, 1985), 431.

3. Edward K. Kaplan, *Holiness in Words: Abraham Joshua Heschel's Poetics of Piety* (Albany, NY: State University of New York Press, 1996), 116, cited from "No Man Is an Island," in *Union Seminary Quarterly Review* 21, no. 2 (January 1966): 117-34.

4. Elie Wiesel, *All Rivers Run to the Sea: Memoirs* (New York: Alfred A. Knopf, 1995), 353.

5. Ibid.

6. Ibid., 354.

7. Kaplan, *Holiness in Words,* 166.

8. Ibid., 99.

9. Shannon, *The Hidden Ground of Love,* 430.

10. Kaplan, *Holiness in Words,* 115.

11. Ibid., 154.

12. Abraham Joshua Heschel, *God in Search of Man: A Philosophy of Judaism* (New York: Harper and Row, 1955), 137.

13. Ibid., 141.

14. Ibid., 136–41.

15. Thomas Merton, *New Seeds of Contemplation* (New York: New Directions, 1961), 130.

16. Heschel, *God in Search of Man,* 141.

17. William H. Shannon, Christine M. Bochen, and Patrick F. O'Connell, eds., *The Thomas Merton Encyclopedia* (Maryknoll, NY: Orbis Books, 2002), 506.

18. Bruteau, *Merton and Judaism,* 224.

19. Ibid.

20. Shannon, *The Hidden Ground of Love,* 434.

21. Ibid., 434–35.

22. Robert E. Daggy, ed., *Dancing in the Water of Life: The Journals of Thomas Merton,* vol. 5, 1963–1965 (New York: Harper Collins, 1997), 142.

23. Shannon, *The Hidden Ground of Love,* 433.

24. Ibid.

25. Ibid., 433–34.

26. Ibid., 433.

27. Brenda Fitch Fairaday, "Thomas Merton's Prophetic Voice: Merton, Heschel and Vatican II," in Bruteau, *Merton and Judaism*, 274.

28. Ibid., 275.

29. Although the Time-Life project on the Bible was never completed and the idea was abandoned by the publishers, Merton's introductory essay was printed in 1970 by The Liturgical Press with the title *Opening the Bible.*

30. Shannon, *The Hidden Ground of Love,* 435.

31. Bruteau, *Merton and Judaism,* 231.

32. Merton, *Opening the Bible,* 7.

33. Ibid., 68–69.

6 Zen: The Merton-Suzuki Letters

1. William H. Shannon, Christine M. Bochen, and Patrick F. O'Connell, eds., *The Thomas Merton Encyclopedia* (Maryknoll, NY: Orbis Books, 2002), 546.

2. William H. Shannon, ed., *The Hidden Ground of Love: The Letters of Thomas Merton on Religious Experience and Social Concerns* (New York: Farrar, Straus and Giroux, 1985), 561.

3. Ibid.

4. Ibid.

5. Robert E. Daggy, ed., *Encounter: Thomas Merton and D. T. Suzuki* (Louisville, KY: Larkspur Press, 1988), 11.

6. D. T. Suzuki, *An Introduction to Zen Buddhism* (New York: Grove Press, 1964), 45.

7. Ibid.

8. Shannon, *The Hidden Ground of Love,* 561.

9. Mircea Eliade, ed., *The Encyclopedia of Religion* (New York: Macmillan, 1987), 14:184.

10. Ibid.

11. D. T. Suzuki, *Outlines of Mahayana Buddhism* (New York: Schocken Books, 1963), 195.

12. Shannon, *The Hidden Ground of Love,* 126.

13. D. T. Suzuki, *An Introduction to Zen Buddhism* (New York: Grove Press, 1964), 44.

14. Eliade, *The Encyclopedia of Religion,* 14:185.

15. Ibid.

16. Shannon, *The Hidden Ground of Love,* 562.

17. Shannon, Bochen, and O'Connell, *The Thomas Merton Encyclopedia,* 461.

18. Thomas Merton, *Zen and the Birds of Appetite* (New York: New Directions, 1968), 103.

19. Ibid., 36.

20. Shannon, *The Hidden Ground of Love,* 563.

21. Ibid.

22. Ibid., 564.

23. Ibid.

24. Ibid.

25. Ibid.

26. Merton, *Zen and the Birds of Appetite,* 35.

27. Daggy, *Encounter,* 47.

28. Ibid.

29. Ibid.

30. Shannon, Bochen, and O'Connell, *The Thomas Merton Encyclopedia,* 461.

31. Mihoko Okamura, on behalf of D. T. Suzuki, to Merton, June 1, 1964, archives of the Thomas Merton Center, Bellarmine University, Louisville, Kentucky.

32. Daggy, *Encounter,* 57.

33. Ibid., 117.

34. Merton, *Zen and the Birds of Appetite,* 59.

7 Openness: The Merton-Hinson Letters

1. John Eudes Bamberger, quoted in Brother Patrick Hart, ed., *Thomas Merton, Monk: A Monastic Tribute,* enl. ed. (Kalamazoo, MI: Cistercian Publications, 1983), 39.

2. For information on these invited and uninvited guests, see Michael Mott, *The Seven Mountains of Thomas Merton* (Boston: Houghton Mifflin, 1984), esp. 517.

3. Robert E. Daggy, ed., *Dancing in the Water of Life* (San Francisco: Harper San Francisco, 1997), 153.

4. For a good sense of Merton's retreat from the world and return to the world read William H. Shannon, *Silent Lamp: The Thomas Merton Story* (New York: Crossroad, 1993), chaps. 7–10.

5. Thomas Merton, *The Waters of Siloe* (New York: Doubleday Image Books, 1962), 262–63.

6. William H. Shannon, Christine M. Bochen, and Patrick F. O'Connell, eds., *The Thomas Merton Encyclopedia* (Maryknoll, NY: Orbis Books, 2002), 127.

7. Interview with Glenn Hinson, Louisville, October 2003. Hinson shared many memories of Thomas Merton, beginning with Hinson's own desire to expose his students to the Abbey of Gethsemani so they could learn about Catholic monastic life, which was central to his courses on church history and Christian spirituality.

8. William H. Shannon, ed., *The Hidden Ground of Love: The Letters of Thomas Merton on Religious Experience and Social Concerns* (New York: Farrar, Straus and Giroux, 1985), 396.

9. Shannon, Bochen, and O'Connell, *The Thomas Merton Encyclopedia,* 127.

10. Glenn Hinson to Merton, November 18, 1964, archives of the Thomas Merton Center, Bellarmine University, Louisville, Kentucky (hereafter TMC).

11. Thomas Merton, *The Seven Storey Mountain* (New York: Harcourt Brace Jovanovich, 1948), 208.

12. Ibid., 57.

13. Ibid., 119.

14. Glenn Hinson, "Expansive Catholicism: Ecumenical Perspectives on Thomas Merton," *Cistercian Studies* 14, no. 3 (1979), quoted in Brother Patrick Hart, *The Message of Thomas Merton* (Kalamazoo, MI: Cistercian Press, 1981), 56.

15. Ibid., 64.

16. Email received from Glenn Hinson, September 25, 2004. In this note Hinson shared with me his own perspective on what I call his expansive Protestantism. He found my assessment of his spiritual development to be accurate.

17. Ibid.

18. Glenn Hinson considered Douglas Steere one of his most important mentors. He has written a biography of Steere entitled *Love at the Heart of Things: A Biography of Douglas V. Steere* (Wallingford, PA: Pendle Hill, 1997).

19. Hinson to Merton, November 18, 1964 (TMC).

20. Interview with Hinson, October 2004.

21. Merton to Hinson, May 8, 1961 (TMC).

22. Shannon, Bochen, and O'Connell, *The Thomas Merton Encyclopedia*, 127.

23. Ibid.

24. This information is contained in a letter from December 24, 2004, sent to me by Glenn Hinson after reviewing a draft of this chapter.

25. Merton to Hinson, December 22, 1962 (TMC).

26. For evidence of Merton's multicultural experiences, see Mott, *The Seven Mountains of Thomas Merton*, esp. chaps. 1–3.

27. Hinson to Merton, September 12, 1967 (TMC).

28. Shannon, Bochen, and O'Connell, *The Thomas Merton Encyclopedia*, 509.

29. Hinson to Merton, September 12, 1967 (TMC).

30. Ibid.

31. Ibid.

8 Compassion: The Merton–Nhat Hanh Letters

1. Robert Ellsberg, ed., *Thich Nhat Hanh: Essential Writings* (Maryknoll, NY, Orbis Books, 2001), 1.

2. Robert H. King, *Thomas Merton and Thich Nhat Hanh* (New York: Continuum, 2003), 72.

3. Ibid.

4. Ibid., 73.

5. Ibid., 74.

6. Thomas Merton, *Mysticism and Zen Masters* (New York: Dell Publishing Co., 1979), 286.

7. Ibid., 285–86.

8. Ibid., 286.

9. Thich Nhat Hanh, *Vietnam: Lotus in a Sea of Fire* (New York: Hill and Wang, 1967), 57.

10. King, *Thomas Merton and Thich Nhat Hanh*, 76.

11. Ibid., 84.

12. Merton's insistence that Christians identify with the world's sufferings can be found in many of his works, of course. *Conjectures of a Guilty Bystander* may provide the best collection of essays on this theme. See Thomas Merton, *Conjectures of a Guilty Bystander* (Garden City, NY: Doubleday, 1966).

13. Both Thich Nhat Hanh and Thomas Merton seemed especially familiar with Dietrich Bonhoeffer's *Letters and Papers from Prison*, taken from his reflections from prison prior to his hanging by the Gestapo in April of 1945.

14. Thomas Merton, *Faith and Violence* (Notre Dame, IN: University of Notre Dame Press, 1968), 13.

15. Thich Nhat Hanh, *Love in Action: Writings in Nonviolent Social Change* (Berkeley, CA: Parallax Press, 1993), 39.

16. Ibid.

17. "Nhat Hanh Is My Brother" is available in several sources. Perhaps the best context for it is provided in *Passion for Peace: The Social Essays of Thomas Merton,* ed. William H. Shannon (New York: Crossroad, 1997), a very thoughtful arrangement of some of Thomas Merton's key essays on social issues related to peace.

18. William H. Shannon, Christine M. Bochen, and Patrick F. O'Connell, eds., *The Thomas Merton Encyclopedia* (Maryknoll, NY: Orbis Books, 2002), 509.

19. Shannon, *Passion for Peace*, 260–62.

20. Ibid.

21. Ibid.

22. King, *Thomas Merton and Thich Nhat Hanh*, 85.

23. Ibid.

24. William H. Shannon, ed., *The Hidden Ground of Love* (New York: Farrar, Straus and Giroux, 1985), 382.

25. Thich Nhat Hanh to Merton, September 3, 1966, archives of the Thomas Merton Center, Bellarmine University, Louisville, Kentucky (hereafter TMC).

26. Shannon, *The Hidden Ground of Love*, 382.

27. Ibid., 381.

28. King, *Thomas Merton and Thich Nhat Hanh*, 85.

29. Merton to Thich Nhat Hanh, June 29, 1966 (TMC).

30. Thich Nhat Hanh to Merton, September 3, 1966 (TMC).

31. Ibid.

9 Courage: The Merton-Yungblut Letters

1. Thomas Merton, *Seeds of Destruction* (New York: Farrar, Straus and Giroux, 1964), 36.

2. June J. Yungblut, *This Is the Child* (Tucson, AZ: Mettler Studios, 1975), page not numbered.

3. Michael Mott, *The Seven Mountains of Thomas Merton* (New York: Harcourt Brace and Company, 1984), 519.

4. William H. Shannon, ed., *The Hidden Ground of Love: The Letters of Thomas Merton on Religious Experience and Social Concerns* (New York: Farrar, Straus and Giroux, 1985), 644.

5. Ibid., 645.

6. Ibid., 451.

7. June J. Yungblut to Merton, April 11, 1968, archives of the Thomas Merton Center, Bellarmine University, Louisville, Kentucky (hereafter TMC).

8. Ibid.

9. Martin Luther King, Jr., *Strength to Love* (Philadelphia: Fortress Press, 1963). This collection of sermons by Dr. King preached at either the Dexter Avenue Baptist Church of Montgomery, Alabama, or the Ebenezer Baptist Church of Atlanta, Georgia, is often considered his most influential book. Coretta Scott King reports in her 1982 foreword to the book that people constantly told her this book "changed their lives."

10. June J. Yungblut to Merton, March 2, 1968 (TMC).

11. William H. Shannon, Christine M. Bochen, and Patrick F. O'Connell, eds., *The Thomas Merton Encyclopedia* (Maryknoll, NY: Orbis Books, 2002), 199.

12. Ibid.

13. Thomas Merton, "Preface," *The Seven Storey Mountain*, Japanese ed., quoted in Henri Nouwen, *Encounters with Merton* (New York: Crossroad, 2003), 107.

14. Shannon, *The Hidden Ground of Love,* 638.

15. Shannon, Bochen, and O'Connell, *The Thomas Merton Encyclopedia,* 86.

16. The best testimony to Merton's ability to encourage others can be found in the witness of his many friends who contributed to Paul Wilkes, ed., *Merton by Those Who Knew Him Best* (San Francisco: Harper and Row, 1984).

17. June J. Yungblut to Merton, March 2, 1968 (TMC).

18. Ibid.

19. Shannon, *The Hidden Ground of Love,* 641.

20. In *Conjectures of a Guilty Bystander* Merton's mention of Dietrich Bonhoeffer's work suggests his familiarity with Bonhoeffer's concept of cheap grace and costly grace. The genuine expression of God's love is indeed costly to God, as revealed in Christ, and to those who seek to follow in the way of Christ's love. See Thomas Merton, *Conjectures of a Guilty Bystander* (Garden City, NY: Doubleday and Company, 1966), 319.

21. King, *Strength to Love,* 5.

22. Ibid.

10 Unity: The Merton–Dona Luisa Coomaraswamy Letters

1. Lawrence S. Cunningham, ed., *Thomas Merton: Spiritual Master* (New York: Paulist Press, 1992), 229.

2. Ibid.

3. For a very helpful summary of Ananda K. Coomaraswamy's life and work, see Roger Lipsey, "Ananda Coomaraswamy," in *The Encyclopedia of Religion,* 2nd ed., ed. Lindsay Jones (New York: Macmillan Reference, 2005), 3:1974.
7), 14: .

4. Ananda K. Coomaraswamy, *The Dance of Shiva* (New York: Noonday Press, 1957), 5.

5. Lipsey, "Ananda Coomaraswamy," 3:1974.

6. Ananda K. Coomaraswamy, *Am I My Brother's Keeper?* (Freeport, NY: Books for Libraries Press, 1967), 45.

7. Ibid.

8. Ibid.

9. Ibid., 50.

10. Ibid.

11. Dona Luisa Coomaraswamy to Merton, December 24, 1960, archives of the Thomas Merton Center, Bellarmine University, Louisville, Kentucky (hereafter TMC).

12. For an important discussion of the establishment of the Thomas Merton Trust and Merton's concerns for his writings and the ambivalence he expresses about how he might be remembered, see Michael Mott, *The Seven Mountains of Thomas Merton* (Boston: Houghton Mifflin, 1984), 499–502.

13. William H. Shannon, ed., *The Hidden Ground of Love: The Letters of Thomas Merton on Religious Experience and Social Concern* (New York: Farrar, Straus and Giroux, 1985). 126–27.

14. Ibid., 125.

15. Ibid., 127.

16. Ibid.

17. Ibid.

18. Coomaraswamy, *The Dance of Shiva,* 4.

19. Ibid.

20. Dona Luisa Coomaraswamy to Merton, January 23, 1961 (TMC).

21. Shannon, *The Hidden Ground of Love,* 128.

22. Ibid., 128–29.

23. Ibid.

24. Merton to Dona Luisa Coomaraswamy, February 12, 1961 (TMC).

25. Coomaraswamy, *The Dance of Shiva,* 1.

26. Dona Luisa Coomaraswamy to Merton, January 23, 1961 (TMC).

27. Shannon, *The Hidden Ground of Love,* 128.

28. Ibid.

29. Ibid.

30. Dona Luisa Coomaraswamy to Merton, January 23, 1961 (TMC).

31. Ibid.

32. Shannon, *The Hidden Ground of Love,* 127.

33. Ibid., 132.

34. Ibid., 133.

35. Dona Luisa Coomaraswamy to Merton, September 1, 1961 (TMC).

36. Robert E. Daggy, ed., *The Road to Joy* (New York: Farrar, Straus and Giroux, 1989), 26.

Postscript

1. Naomi Burton Stone, Brother Patrick Hart, and James Laughlin, eds., *The Asian Journal of Thomas Merton* (New York: New Directions, 1973), 308.

Bibliography

Baker, Rob, and Gray Henry, eds. *Merton and Sufism: The Untold Story.* Louisville, KY: Fons Vitae, 1999.

Bochen, Christine M. *Thomas Merton: Essential Writings.* Maryknoll, NY: Orbis Books, 2002.

Bruteau, Beatrice, ed. *Merton and Judaism: Holiness in Words.* Louisville, KY: Fons Vitae, 2003.

Burton, Naomi, Br. Patrick Hart, and James Laughlin, eds. *The Asian Journal of Thomas Merton.* New York: New Directions, 1973.

Coomaraswamy, Ananda K. *Am I My Brother's Keeper?* Freeport, NY: Books for Libraries Press, 1947.

——. *The Dance of Shiva.* New York: Noonday Press, 1957.

Cunningham, Lawrence S., ed. *Thomas Merton: Spiritual Master.* New York: Paulist Press, 1992.

Daggy, Robert E., ed. *Encounter: Thomas Merton and D. T. Suzuki.* Louisville, KY: Larkspur Press, 1988.

——, ed. *Dancing in the Waters of Life: The Journals of Thomas Merton.* New York: Harper Collins, 1997.

Eliade, Mircea, ed. *The Encyclopedia of Religion.* New York: Macmillan, 1987.

Hart, Br. Patrick. *The Message of Thomas Merton.* Kalamazoo, MI: Cistercian Press, 1981.

——, ed. *Thomas Merton, Monk: A Monastic Tribute.* Enlarged edition. Kalamazoo, MI: Cistercian Publications, 1983.

Heschel, Abraham Joshua. *God in Search of Man: A Philosophy of Judaism.* New York: Harper and Row, 1955.

Kaplan, Edward K. *Holiness in Words: Abraham Joshua Heschel's Poetics of Piety.* Albany, NY: State University of New York Press, 1996.

King, Martin Luther, Jr. *Strength to Love.* Philadelphia: Fortress Press, 1963.

King, Robert H. *Thomas Merton and Thich Nhat Hanh.* New York: Continuum, 2003.

Merton, Thomas. *Conjectures of a Guilty Bystander.* Garden City, NY: Doubleday, 1966.

———. *Faith and Violence.* Notre Dame, IN: University of Notre Dame Press, 1968.

———. *Gandhi on Non-Violence.* New York: New Directions, 1965.

———. *New Seeds of Contemplation.* New York: New Directions, 1961.

———. *Opening the Bible.* Collegeville, MN: Liturgical Press, 1970.

———. *Seeds of Destruction.* New York: Farrar, Straus and Giroux, 1964.

———. *The Seven Storey Mountain.* New York: Harcourt Brace Jovanovich, 1948.

———. *The Waters of Siloe.* New York: Doubleday Image Books, 1962.

———. *The Way of Chuang Tzu.* New York: New Directions, 1965.

———. *Zen and the Birds of Appetite.* New York: New Directions, 1968.

Mott, Michael. *The Seven Mountains of Thomas Merton.* Boston: Houghton Mifflin, 1984.

Nouwen, Henri. *Encounters with Merton.* New York: Crossroad, 2004.

Shannon, William H., ed. *The Hidden Ground of Love: The Letters of Thomas Merton on Religious Experience and Social Concerns.* New York: Farrar, Straus and Giroux, 1985.

———. *Passion for Peace: The Social Essays of Thomas Merton.* New York: Crossroad, 1997.

———, ed. *Silent Lamp: The Thomas Merton Story.* New York: Crossroad, 1993.

Shannon, William H., Christine M. Bochen, and Patrick F. O'Connell, eds. *The Thomas Merton Encyclopedia.* Maryknoll, NY: Orbis Books, 2002.

Suzuki, D. T. *An Introduction to Zen Buddhism.* New York: Grove Press, 1964.

———. *Outlines of Mahayana Buddhism.* New York: Schocken Books, 1963.

Wiesel, Elie. *All Rivers Run to the Sea: Memoirs.* New York: Alfred A. Knopf, 1995.

Wilkes, Paul, ed. *Merton by Those Who Knew Him.* New York: Harper and Row, 1984.

Wu, John C. H. *Beyond East and West.* New York: Sheed and Ward; Taipei; Mei Ya Publications, 1969.

Yungblut, June J. *This Is the Child.* Tucson, AZ: Mettler Studios, 1975.